W9-AJK-867

WORLD HISTORY

THE
BRITISH
MONARCHY

THE CHANGING ROLE OF THE ROYAL FAMILY

By Nicole Horning

Portions of this book originally appeared in *The British Monarchy* by Andrew A. Kling.

LUCENT PRESS

Published in 2020 by
Lucent Press, an Imprint of Greenhaven Publishing, LLC
353 3rd Avenue
Suite 255
New York, NY 10010

Designer: Deanna Paternostro
Editor: Diane Bailey

Library of Congress Cataloging-in-Publication Data

Names: Horning, Nicole, author.
Title: The British monarchy : the changing role of the royal family / Nicole
  Horning.
Description: First edtion. | New York : Lucent Press, [2020] | Series: World
  history | Includes bibliographical references and index.
Identifiers: LCCN 2019001040 (print) | LCCN 2019004527 (ebook) | ISBN
  9781534567825 (eBook) | ISBN 9781534567818 (pbk. book) | ISBN
  9781534567139 (library bound book)
Subjects: LCSH: Great Britain–Kings and rulers–Biography. | Monarchy–Great
  Britain–History.
Classification: LCC DA28.1 (ebook) | LCC DA28.1 .H67 2020 (print) | DDC
  941.009/9–dc23
LC record available at https://lccn.loc.gov/2019001040

Printed in the United States of America

CPSIA compliance information: Batch #BS19KL: For further information contact Greenhaven Publishing LLC, New York, New York at 1-844-317-7404.

Please visit our website, www.greenhavenpublishing.com. For a free color catalog of all our high-quality books, call toll free 1-844-317-7404 or fax 1-844-317-7405.

Contents

Foreword

History books are often filled with names and dates—words and numbers for students to memorize for a test and forget once they move on to another class. However, what history books should be filled with are great stories, because the history of our world is filled with great stories. Love, death, violence, heroism, and betrayal are not just themes found in novels and movie scripts. They are often the driving forces behind major historical events.

When told in a compelling way, fact is often far more interesting—and sometimes far more unbelievable—than fiction. World history is filled with more drama than the best television shows, and all of it really happened. As readers discover the incredible truth behind the triumphs and tragedies that have impacted the world since ancient times, they also come to understand that everything is connected. Historical events do not exist in a vacuum. The stories that shaped world history continue to shape the present and will undoubtedly shape the future.

The titles in this series aim to provide readers with a comprehensive understanding of pivotal events in world history. They are written with a focus on providing readers with multiple perspectives to help them develop an appreciation for the complexity of the study of history. There is no set lens through which history must be viewed, and these titles encourage readers to analyze different viewpoints to understand why a historical figure acted the way they did or why a contemporary scholar wrote what they did about a historical event. In this way, readers are able to sharpen their critical-thinking skills and apply those skills in their history classes. Readers are aided in this pursuit by formally documented quotations and annotated bibliographies, which encourage further research and debate.

Many of these quotations come from carefully selected primary sources, including diaries, public records, and contemporary research and writings. These valuable primary sources help readers hear the voices of those who directly experienced historical events, as well as the voices of biographers and historians who provide a unique perspective on familiar topics. Their voices all help history come alive in a vibrant way.

As students read the titles in this series, they are provided with clear context in the form of maps, timelines, and informative text. These elements give them the basic facts they need to fully appreciate the high drama that is history.

The study of history is difficult at times—not because of all the information that needs to be memorized, but because of the challenging questions it asks us. How could something as horrible as the Holocaust happen? What are the roots of the struggle for peace in the Middle East? Why are some people reluctant to call themselves feminists? The information presented in each title gives readers the tools they need to confront these questions and participate in the debates they inspire.

As we pore over the stories of events and eras that changed the world, we come to understand a simple truth: No one can escape being a part of history. We are not bystanders; we are active participants in the stories that are being created now and will be written about in history books decades and even centuries from now. The titles in this series help readers gain a deeper appreciation for history and a stronger understanding of the connection between the stories of the past and the stories they are part of right now.

SETTING THE SCENE: A TIMELINE

1837 ···· **1901** ···· **1910** ···· **1917** ···· **1936** ···· **1952** ····

King George VI assumes power after his brother, Edward VIII, abdicates the throne.

Queen Victoria dies, ending a nearly 64-year reign, a record that lasted until Queen Elizabeth.

King George V replaces the name of Saxe-Coburg-Gotha with House of Windsor.

King George VI dies; his daughter Elizabeth becomes queen.

Queen Victoria ascends to the throne. The era of her reign becomes known as the Victorian Age.

King George V ascends to the throne.

| 1981 | 2011 | 2013 | 2015 | 2017 | 2018 |

Kate Middleton gives birth to her and Prince William's first child, Prince George.

Queen Elizabeth celebrates 65 years on the throne with her Sapphire Jubilee; she is the first monarch in British history to reach this milestone.

Prince William and Kate Middleton marry on April 29.

Princess Charlotte, the second child of Kate Middleton and Prince William, is born in May.

Kate Middleton gives birth to her and Prince William's third child, Louis Arthur Charles, in April. Prince Harry marries Meghan Markle in May; in October, they announce they are expecting their first child, due in spring 2019.

Prince Charles and Lady Diana Spencer are married. They later have two children, Prince William and Prince Harry.

A SENSE OF TRADITION

The British monarchy has fascinated people worldwide for years. In 2011, nearly 23 million people in the United States watched the wedding of Prince William Arthur Philip Louis to Catherine (commonly called Kate) Middleton on television. A few years later, in 2018, the wedding of Prince Henry ("Harry") Charles Albert David to Meghan Markle drew more than 29 million viewers in the United States alone. Television shows such as *The Crown* also reflect the popularity of the monarchy.

Being enamored with the people and actions of the British monarchy is not just a recent fad. According to Boston University history professor Arianne Chernock, the American interest in the British monarchy "has been alive pretty much since 1776. Pretty much as soon as we severed ties, we were back to being fascinated—captivated really—by the royal family."[1] This interest tends to increase during important and highly publicized events such as the births of children, weddings, funerals, royal visits, and the coronation—the ceremony formally giving the monarch regal power—of a new ruler.

The crowning of Queen Elizabeth II in 1953 was groundbreaking. Her coronation was the first one to be televised, and 27 million people in the United Kingdom (UK) and millions more worldwide watched the event. With this event, Elizabeth was crowned queen of the United Kingdom of Great Britain and Northern Ireland.

Almost 30 years later, in 1981, the wedding of Prince Charles Philip Arthur George to Lady Diana Spencer was one of the most watched events on television in the 1980s. Then, in 1997, when Diana died in a car accident, the entire world mourned. About

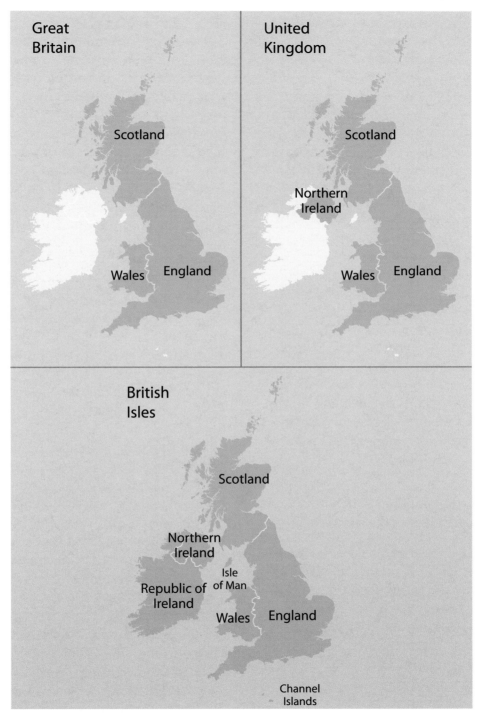

Great
Britain

Scotland

Wales England

United
Kingdom

Scotland

Northern
Ireland

Wales England

British
Isles

Scotland

Northern
Ireland

Isle
of Man

Republic of
Ireland

Wales England

Channel
Islands

Elizabeth II is Queen of the United Kingdom of Great Britain and Northern Ireland. Great Britain is made up of Scotland, England, and Wales.

30 million people in the United States watched the funeral.

The lives of wealthy, powerful people are always of interest to the public, but Americans' curiosity about the British monarchy goes deeper than that, according to Jeff Rudski, an assistant professor in the psychology department at Muhlenberg College in Allentown, Pennsylvania. He said,

> Royals touch upon something more primal. Our need for identity motivates us to explore our past. They connect us to history and to tradition in a very simple and tangible way. Historically, they were major contributors to world events … While royals no longer play such major historical roles, the direct lineage is, in a way, an easy-to-follow connection to the past. People often like to romanticize the past, and what can be more romantic than the sagas of kings and queens.[2]

Chernock added that the royals have a unique place in the social order:

> These are people who haven't chosen this life for themselves. With the exception of those who marry into the family, they're born into it, and they have to make the best of those circumstances, which are difficult circumstances. That puts them in a different category of celebrity. This is a lifelong undertaking that they have to figure out as they go along.[3]

The Peerage System

Today, the government of Britain operates as a constitutional monarchy. Elected officials make political decisions, while the monarch (the king or queen) acts as the head of state but only makes decisions upon the advice of Parliament or other officials. This system reflects changes that have occurred over the years. In the past, the monarch had supreme power, but the system gradually shifted to become more democratic.

In a monarchy, the position of king or queen can only be assumed through heredity, or being born into the royal family. This system of inheritance prioritizes the oldest child, and this child is assumed to be an heir to the throne. For many years in Britain, the oldest son inherited the throne, but now, the oldest child—regardless of gender—inherits the throne.

Members of the British monarchy also have royal titles, which they acquire through the peerage system. The media often incorrectly use terms such as king, queen, princess, and prince. For example, Kate Middleton's correct title is the Duchess of Cambridge, but some people mistakenly call her "Princess Kate."

Queen Elizabeth's four children have the title of princess and prince, but they also have other titles. When men of the royal family get married, they are often given new titles. Upon marrying Kate Middleton, for example, William went from being His Royal Highness Prince

The system of inheritance prioritizes the eldest child. The next in line to the British throne is Prince Charles (second from left), and then Prince William (second from right) is next in line after him.

William of Wales to the Duke of Cambridge. When Harry married Meghan Markle, he was given the title of Duke of Sussex, and Meghan became the Duchess of Sussex.

The highest ranking is queen or king. This person has the power to give titles such as duke, earl, and more to others. Following the king or queen, the next highest ranking is queen consort. This person is married to the king and is often called simply a queen, but she has no power. While it seems this system would make Queen Elizabeth II's husband, Philip, a king or a king consort, that is not the case. In the UK, men who are married to the monarch are given the title of prince consort.

Following the queen consort are the titles of prince and princess. A prince or princess is the child of the monarch, which is why calling Kate a princess is incorrect—in order to have the title of prince or princess, she would have had to be born into the royal family. Lady Diana Spencer also was incorrectly called Princess Diana—her correct title was Diana, Princess of Wales. She was referred to as a princess because when a woman marries a royal family member, she adopts her husband's title.

The next title is when the peerage titles start. The highest role in the peerage system is a duke or duchess. Both Harry and William are dukes. The second degree in the peerage system is marquess or marchioness. This role was created for nobles who held land on the border territories of the Scottish and Welsh marshes. Next comes

Kate (left) and Diana (right) have both incorrectly been called "Princess." They would have had to be born into the royal family to officially have the title of Princess.

an earl or, for a woman, a countess. This rank is generally inherited from the father.

The next degree in the peerage system is the viscount or viscountess. This person is generally the child of an earl, and therefore inherits the title. However, it can also be granted. The lowest rank in the peerage system is a baron or baroness; this rank is also generally inherited.

Marquesses, earls, viscounts, and barons can all be called "lord" or "lady" instead of by their full title. Additionally, a person can have multiple titles. For example, William's full title is His Royal Highness Prince William Arthur Philip Louis, Duke of Cambridge, Earl of Strathearn, Baron Carrickfergus, Royal Knight Companion of the Most Noble Order of the Garter.

A Growing Controversy

Being part of the royal family does not simply mean getting a title, however. Close family members of Queen Elizabeth take on official duties when the queen cannot be there in person. These duties include attending events both in the UK and abroad; each year, the family is committed to more than 2,000 official engagements. Additionally, the royal family helps others through a wide variety of charitable organizations that support health care, education, the environment, and more.

While the monarchy has been entrenched in British society for hundreds of years, there is an increasing amount of controversy over whether it is needed or appropriate in the modern world. Those who believe it should change oppose the institution for various reasons, one of which is because its leader is not elected.

There is also tremendous pressure on spouses who marry into the family and find their lives drastically changed by their new role and responsibilities. For example, when Meghan Markle married Prince Harry, she gave up her acting career.

The most important reason people oppose the monarchy concerns the distribution of wealth. At a time of housing crises and decreasing incomes, the royal family lives in palaces and puts on elaborate weddings—which are funded by taxpayers. William and Kate's wedding, for example, cost around $34 million. This inequality results in many people opposing the monarchy, what it stands for, and its use of money. However, the long tradition of the monarchy is hard to break, and many British citizens respect the position of the royal family and cherish its contribution to their country's history.

CHAPTER ONE

THE MONARCHY IN MEDIEVAL ENGLAND

The British monarchy is an institution that dates back to medieval England and the rule of Alfred the Great, who was named king of Wessex in the year 871. At a time when Vikings were raiding England, Alfred led successful military campaigns against them and set up a program of defense settlements in which settlers were given plots of land and would defend them during times of war. His kingship extended beyond Wessex and eventually took on greater significance. Alfred also established legal codes and arranged for the translation of books about philosophy, history, and geography. According to the official website of the royal family, Alfred's reign was important for establishing the future British monarchy:

> By stopping the Viking advance and consolidating his territorial gains, Alfred had started the process by which his successors eventually extended their power over the other Anglo-Saxon kings; the ultimate unification of Anglo-Saxon England was to be led by Wessex.
>
> It is for his valiant defence of his kingdom against a stronger enemy, for securing peace with the Vikings and for his farsighted reforms in the reconstruction of Wessex and beyond, that Alfred—alone of all the English kings and queens—is known as "the Great." [4]

Viking Raiders

The Vikings, from present-day Norway, Sweden, and Denmark, had been raiding England since the 790s, sending fast-moving armies numbering in the thousands. These raids eventually resulted in the creation of permanent settlements. In 866, Vikings seized the English city of York and established a kingdom in Northumbria, the larger area around York. The areas of Mercia and East Anglia were also invaded and

King Alfred is the only British king who is referred to as "the Great." A statue of him is shown here.

occupied by the Danes—people from Denmark. In 870, they attacked Wessex. At the time, Wessex was the last independent Anglo-Saxon kingdom. In 871, at the Battle of Ashdown in Berskshire, England made an important stand when Alfred defeated the Danes, becoming king of Wessex that year. Alfred went on to lead several successful military campaigns against the Danes and eventually established a peaceful relationship with them.

Today, Alfred is remembered not only for his success against the Viking invaders, but also for his efficient management of his lands, maintaining peace with his neighbors, and initiating a widespread campaign of education. Alfred married the daughter of a Mercian nobleman, and Alfred's grandson, Athelstan, ruled from 924 to 927 as king of the Anglo-Saxons. Athelstan united Wessex and Mercia against the Danes, who ruled in East Anglia. He declared himself "King of the English," and his descendants brought the kingdoms of East Anglia and Northumbria under English rule as well. At the same time, Viking raiders had conquered a territory in the northern part of modern France, which they called Normandy.

By the middle of the 11th century, the kings of England had firm control over the southern part of the island that is now called Great Britain. England's king, Edward, was the son of King Ethelred the Unready (Alfred's great-great-grandson) and his second wife, Emma. She was the daughter of Robert I,

Count of Normandy. Edward, therefore, was half Norman, and in fact, he had spent much of his youth in Normandy. He was known as "the Confessor" because of his deep religious convictions, and he was committed to Christianity and to expanding the Catholic Church's presence in his kingdom. However, Edward had no children, and as he grew older, two men, Harold Godwinson, Earl of Wessex, and William, Duke of Normandy, began to lay plans for claiming the crown of England for themselves after Edward died.

A Fight for the Throne

When Edward died in January 1066, the most powerful families in England gave their allegiance to Harold, and he was crowned king of England almost immediately. Harold had been one of Edward's most effective administrators and his most powerful military leader, and many considered him the natural heir to the throne. However, in Normandy, William prepared to claim the throne for himself.

William's claim was not only based on a desire for power. According to William, when he had visited Edward in 1065, the aging king assured William that he would be king when Edward died. Like Edward, William was also related to Ethelred and Emma; William's grandfather was Emma's brother. This made William and Edward cousins.

William, however, was the illegitimate son of Robert the Magnificent, Duke of Normandy. When Robert died in 1035, William was only seven or eight years old. He inherited his father's lands, and by the time he reached his early 30s, he was a battle-tested leader who had defeated many of his regional rivals. William was upset when Harold was named king, but he bided his time. He planned to claim the throne, but he also wanted to be as prepared as possible and waited until he thought the time was right.

Finally, William assembled an army and a fleet of ships to invade England. In October 1066, he landed on England's southern coast and faced little opposition. Harold was in northern England, fighting a Viking invasion, when he learned of William's landing. After defeating the Vikings, Harold led his army to the southern coast where William was waiting. After a long day of fighting at the Battle of Hastings on October 14, Harold and his brothers were killed on the battlefield, and his remaining army fled. William and his army made the long journey to London, defeating resistance along the way before he claimed the throne. He was crowned king of England on Christmas Day 1066. Since that time, 1066 has been called "the year of three kings," and William of Normandy became known as William the Conqueror.

William's Rule

During William's reign from 1066 to 1087, he solidified his hold on England while simultaneously ruling Normandy. He defeated a series of English revolts and granted territories that had been confiscated from defeated nobles to Norman barons who had supported his claim to the throne. William had several hundred wooden castles built across England to protect his allies against further rebellious attacks. He forced the Norman language and political practices on the kingdom and commissioned the creation of the Bayeux Tapestry, which depicts his invasion of England and victory at Hastings. The Bayeux Tapestry still exists to this day.

William wrote his will to designate his oldest son, Robert, as Duke of Normandy, granting him rule over the French part of his dominion. His youngest son, Henry, was expected to join the Church and was therefore given a good education. William also imported a European tradition into England when he designated an heir to the English throne: his second son, also named William.

William II became king when his father died in 1087. He was eager to keep a firm hold on England, but his support among many of his father's allies was uncertain. For helping the Conqueror's cause, they had received territories in England while also owning lands in Normandy.

However, relations between William and his brother Robert were tense, and when Norman barons in England rebelled against William, Robert stayed in France. Despite Robert's lack of assistance, William fought off the challenge and defeated the rebels. He also

William the Conqueror, crowned on Christmas Day 1066, became England's first Norman king.

The Bayeux Tapestry was commissioned almost 1,000 years ago. A section of it is shown here.

reached accords with Scots leaders to the north and Welsh leaders to the west to help keep the peace. When William II died in a hunting accident in 1100, some historians believed that his younger brother Henry, who was also hunting in the area, had arranged the king's death. Historians have drawn this conclusion because it was Henry, not his older brother Robert, who seized the throne. William II left behind a legacy as a skilled campaigner and an effective administrator, but his brother Henry surpassed both William and their father in consolidating Norman rule in England during the next 35 years.

The Reign of Henry I

In 1096, Duke Robert joined the First Crusade. The Crusades were military expeditions organized by the Church to take back Jerusalem and the Holy Land from the Muslim people who were living there. This same year, four years before William II's death, Duke Robert had turned over Normandy to William

WILLIAM'S INQUEST

Nineteen years after taking power, on Christmas Day 1085, William the Conqueror sent commissioners of inquiry throughout England to learn all they could about the kingdom. They were instructed to find out who held the land, who lived on that land, what property was built on it, how much it was worth, and how much money it generated.

William's inquest involved about 10,000 people and covered 13,418 places. (The major towns of London and Winchester were not included.) The results were presented to him in September 1086. In the centuries that passed, the survey became known as the Domesday Book (pronounced "doomsday"). This written report was considered the official record of the kingdom and was not subject to appeal.

to rule in his absence. Following William's death, news reached England that Robert was returning from the Crusade. A council of the leading barons quickly gathered together and chose Henry as William's successor, in part because Robert had been an ineffective ruler of Normandy. After Robert's bid to win power from Henry failed, it was agreed that Henry would pay Robert an annuity and could remain king of England for his lifetime. However, a few years later, Henry captured Robert and imprisoned him in England for the rest of his life.

Henry I secured his place on the throne by fostering good relations with the Catholic Church. The support of the Church was essential because it had as much power—and maybe more—than Europe's monarchs. A message

of approval or disapproval from the pope in Rome generally dictated who became and stayed king. Henry also made an important political alliance when he married Matilda of Scotland, the daughter of King Malcolm III. They had a successful marriage, as Matilda proved to be an effective administrator over England during Henry's frequent trips to France to deal with Norman affairs. They had two daughters and two sons, and Henry cemented strong bonds with European ruling families by negotiating political marriages for his two eldest children.

Although Henry's military and political successes had placed him in a secure position by 1120, tragedy struck when his two eldest sons, William and Richard, died when a ship on which they were passengers sank shortly after

Henry I's failure to identify a suitable heir before his death resulted in disagreement over who should rule.

leaving Normandy for England. Henry designated his daughter Matilda as his heir, but the English barons were resistant to the idea of being ruled by a woman. An additional stumbling block was that Matilda was married to Geoffrey V, Count of Anjou, who had gotten the nickname "Plantagenet" because he liked to wear in his cap a sprig of the common broom plant with the Latin name *planta genista*. The French domain of Anjou was often at war with Normandy, and the barons did not like the idea of Geoffrey Plantagenet becoming their king.

Henry I died in 1135 having kept the peace in England for 30 years, but he left no heir who the country could agree on as its monarch. As neither Matilda nor Geoffrey moved to take the throne, Henry's nephew Stephen seized the crown.

Count Stephen

Count Stephen of Boulogne was the son of William the Conqueror's daughter Adela and had been Henry I's favorite nephew. When his uncle died, Stephen went to London and immediately gained the support of the people in England's capital city. Stephen was crowned king within three weeks of Henry I's death. The speed of these events took the barons by surprise, but eventually, they recognized Stephen as king of England and Duke of Normandy.

Stephen was popular with the people and was a firm but fair ruler. However, in 1139, Matilda and her half brother, Robert, Duke of Gloucester, began to rebel against Stephen. Matilda and Robert invaded England from France, leading to civil warfare and Stephen's capture and imprisonment in February 1141. Matilda secured the support of the leading barons and the influential bishop of Winchester, and she was called "Lady of the English." Although she was never crowned queen, she was considered the ruler of England. She soon became an unpopular figure, however, because she forced heavy taxes on the nobles and the citizens of London. Stephen's queen, also named Matilda, rallied support to her husband's cause, and the Lady of the English was driven from London. Stephen was released from prison and returned to the throne in November 1141.

Stephen's troubles were not over, though. Those who were loyal to Matilda and Robert continued to challenge Stephen's rule for the next eight years. Robert died in 1147, and Matilda retired to Anjou in 1148, never to return. However, the civil war dragged on in scattered skirmishes before ending in 1149. The final blows to Stephen's reign came in 1153 when his eldest son Eustace died. Henry of Anjou, the son of Matilda and Geoffrey Plantagenet, brought an army to England to force Stephen to recognize Henry's claim to the throne. Through the Treaty of Wallingford, Stephen designated Henry as his heir and successor. Stephen died less than a year later.

Reign of the House of Anjou

After Stephen's death, Henry of Anjou took the throne as Henry II. He established the House of Anjou that would rule England for the next 300 years. Henry II, who reigned from 1154 to 1189, came to the throne of England already ruler of a significant portion of France. He ruled the provinces of Anjou, Maine, and Normandy, as well as Aquitaine through his marriage to Eleanor of Aquitaine. His Angevin realm (the lands ruled by the House of Anjou) stretched from the Scots border in the north to the Pyrenees Mountains in the south, where what are now France and Spain meet.

During Henry's reign, he destroyed many of the castles that had been built during the civil war in order to eliminate their possible use by rivals to challenge his rule. He also introduced a new code of laws. All local courts, which were run by the landowning barons, became subordinate to a new central court, which featured a jury system.

As Henry and Eleanor's four surviving sons became adults and began to seek a role in the empire, their ambitions became part of a complex political game between their parents and each other, which resulted in Henry exiling Eleanor from his court in 1167, allowing only occasional visits to her children on holidays.

Henry had intended to divide his empire among his sons, but fate and politics intervened. His first son had died as a child; the second, Henry (known as the "Young King" since he was the heir apparent), died at 28; and his third son, Geoffrey, was killed in an accident in 1186 at age 27. Only Richard and John were left after this series of events. Richard, the elder son, was Eleanor's favorite, and John was Henry's. Richard formed an alliance with Philip II, the king of France, to invade Henry's French domains, but Henry, now 56, had no energy to fight. The two kings negotiated a peace on July 4, 1189, in which Henry was forced to surrender disputed territories and to acknowledge Richard as his heir. Henry was heartbroken when he discovered that his son John had also helped Philip. He died two days later.

Richard the Lionheart

After his father's death, Richard became king on July 6, 1189. He had been trained as a knight and loved the thrill of the tournament, in which men engaged in one-on-one contests of strength and skill using a variety of weapons, such as the sword and the lance. He had also gained a reputation as a skilled warrior after being in a variety of military campaigns before becoming king.

Richard ruled from 1189 to 1199, yet he spent only six months of that time in England. In December 1189, he joined the Third Crusade, arriving in the Holy Land in 1191. His personality rubbed many of the crusading nobility the wrong way, including one of his allies, Leopold V, Duke of Austria. Richard's army, with the help of Leopold's army and the French, had broken a two-year siege of the town of Acre but failed to recapture Jerusalem from the Islamic armies. England, Austria, and France had all claimed Acre, but Richard had removed Leopold's banner from the town. Leopold, outraged, returned to Europe. Richard's reputation continued to grow as he proved himself both as a fearless warrior and as an innovative leader, gaining the nickname *Coeur de Lion*, or "Lionheart."

However, in 1192, he and several companions were shipwrecked on the shores of the Adriatic Sea (between the modern-day Balkans and Italy) and were forced to travel across Europe on foot to reach home. As they crossed Leopold's domain, they were captured; Richard remained in prison for 15 months while his treasury raised the huge ransom needed for his release. He eventually returned to England in March 1194. There, he found that his brother John, who had been responsible for the French territories, had lost portions of Normandy to Philip II. Richard spent the next five years in France fighting to regain the lost territories and died from wounds sustained in a minor battle there in April 1199.

Today, Richard's abilities on the battlefield are legendary, but his effectiveness as a king continues to be debated by historians. One, John Gillingham, wrote, "By the standards of his own day [Richard] had been an ideal king, preoccupied above all with the crusade and the defense of his ancestral lands," and called him a "generous lord and a shrewd politician."[5] Another historian, Mike Ashley, however, has written that Richard was "an extremely arrogant, petulant king, with a vicious temper and a total lack of moral scruples … He was an excellent soldier … but was useless at anything else."[6]

John I

Richard did not have a son, and upon his death, the crown passed to his brother John, the youngest and last surviving son of Henry II and Eleanor of Aquitaine. John, who reigned from 1199 to 1216, gained the nickname Lackland because his father had already divided his territories among his other sons by the time John was born. As king, he spent almost a decade mounting one military campaign after another to try to maintain the Angevin realms against French expansionism. To finance these wars, John placed a number of heavy taxes on the nobles. The most expensive of these was called scutage, which a baron had to pay when he declined military service. John levied it 11 times over the next 16 years, and paying scutage was soon seen as a measure of a baron's loyalty to the king.

By 1214, the nobles had had enough of John's taxes and military failures. A crushing defeat in France in July and the loss of further territory sent the English barons into open rebellion in May 1215. London soon fell to the rebels, and on June 15, John met with the barons at the small town of Runnymede to negotiate peace. There, he signed a document that history remembers as the Great Charter, more commonly known by its Latin name, the Magna Carta. The charter laid out the specific rights and privileges of the king and of the barons, and it became the basis for the rights of individuals under a government.

However, civil war broke out again as soon as John ignored the charter's provisions and returned to his heavy-handed rule. The rebels pursued John through eastern England, and during this retreat, he developed dysentery and died on October 18, 1216, leaving his son Henry as his heir. John was 46 years old; Henry was only 9.

The Young King Henry III

Nine years old is young to take on

GREAT CHARTER: THE MAGNA CARTA

The Magna Carta, which King John signed in 1215, was designed to put several limits on the king's power. John's barons forced him to sign the document, feeling that John had overstepped the bounds of royal authority. Their intent was to force John to acknowledge restrictions on the king's ability to levy taxes, to respect England's traditional laws and customs, and to recognize a committee that was designed to hold him to that promise.

Over the centuries that followed, the Magna Carta has been used as an example of the idea that both those who are governed and those who govern must obey the law. Its clauses include a number of concepts that still exist in modern law, such as the prohibition against unlawful imprisonment, the right to a speedy trial, and the right to a trial by a jury of one's peers.

the power and responsibilities of a kingship—especially when the kingdom is in the midst of a civil war. Because of his age, Henry III was given regents, or advisors, who had the power to act in the king's name and successfully helped end the civil war.

In 1234, Henry III was old enough to take over and rule on his own, but he proved to be less effective than his regents. There was strain between Henry and his nobles, particularly over the influence some of Henry's relatives had. For example, in 1242, his half brothers involved him in an expensive military campaign. Then, in 1258, a deal with the papacy (the office of the pope) resulted in Henry being threatened with excommunication, or being expelled, from the Catholic Church for not meeting

the financial obligation he had agreed to as part of the deal. Because of this, a 15-member council was selected by the barons to "advise the king and oversee the entire administration. Parliament was to be held three times a year and the households of the king and queen were also to be reformed."[7] However, in 1261, after the barons started to fight among themselves, Henry used the opportunity to state that he was no longer supporting the declarations put forth by the council. Three years later, Simon de Montfort, a baron who opposed Henry, started a rebellion. In April 1264, he captured Henry and his oldest son, Edward. He then ruled England until he was killed in battle by Edward in August 1265. At that point, Henry gave Edward control of the government until Henry's death

Westminster Abbey in London was rebuilt during Henry III's reign. It is the traditional site for coronations of members of the British monarchy.

in 1272. When Henry died, Edward, at 33 years old, was crowned King Edward I.

Although Henry III showed little ability to be an effective leader during his time, some lasting traces of his rule can still be seen today. For example, he paid to have Westminster Abbey rebuilt in the gothic style, and he was buried there. As historian Peter Earle wrote, "Perhaps we give too much glory to our martial kings and too little to those, like Henry III, who have made England a more civilized country."[8]

CHAPTER TWO

THE WARS OF THE ROSES

T he death of Henry III marked a new era. He is labeled as the last Angevin king by some historians and the first Plantagenet king by others. Therefore, his son Edward's ascension to the throne marked the beginning of more than 100 years of kings who were descendants of the Plantagenets of the House of Anjou.

The Scots and Welsh versus Edward I

Unlike his father, Edward I was a grown man when he took the throne. He already had a record of military accomplishments and was well prepared to rule. One of his longest-lasting achievements as king was the reformation of the nation's legal system. Commoners and nobles alike benefited as the rights and obligations of landowners were specifically laid out. Edward also commissioned a thorough survey of the country to resolve disputes over who owned the lands across the realm,

an action that made collecting taxes clearer. He met regularly with Parliament, which after 1295, was composed of the House of Lords (landowners and church leaders) and the House of Commons (elected representatives of the townsfolk and county dwellers). With Parliament's assistance, Edward instituted more reforms over a period of 20 years. According to Mike Ashley, "During this process Edward was quick to punish those who had abused their authority. In this way Edward endeared himself to the commoners of England, who saw him as their saviour."[9]

The people of Scotland and Wales saw Edward in a much different light, holding him responsible for the loss of their independence. The Welsh leader Llywelyn ap Gruffudd refused to appear at Edward's coronation to acknowledge Edward as his king. In 1267, under the Treaty of Montgomery, Henry III had recognized Llywelyn as the Prince of Wales; as such, Llywelyn believed that he did not need to acknowledge Edward. Edward felt otherwise, and he retaliated by leading two campaigns against Llywelyn and his followers in 1277 and again in 1282. Llywelyn was killed in the second confrontation, and Welsh resistance soon crumbled. The Statute of Wales in 1284 brought the territory into Edward's dominion, and he ordered the construction of a ring of castles to protect it. Many of them stand to this day.

While the Welsh resented Edward for their loss of independence, he was absolutely despised by the Scots. In 1291, Edward was invited to mediate a dispute between three nobles who were all making a claim for the vacant Scots throne. Edward decided to take advantage of the situation by demanding that the Scots recognize him as their overlord. By 1296, the situation

Edward I's controversial decisions made him extremely unpopular with the Scots and the Welsh.

had deteriorated into open warfare. In March 1296, Edward stormed and sacked the town of Berwick, and in April, the main Scots army was crushed at the Battle of Dunbar.

These defeats led to the rise of two of Scotland's iconic leaders, William Wallace and Robert the Bruce. Wallace led an army of peasants and outlaws through several campaigns of guerrilla warfare against Edward's army, which defeated Wallace at Falkirk in 1298. A fictionalized story of William Wallace and Edward I is told in the critically acclaimed 1995 movie *Braveheart*, starring Mel Gibson as Wallace.

In 1307, Robert the Bruce's bid for power convinced Edward, now 68, to march north with another army to subdue the Scots. He never made it there, however. He fell ill with dysentery and died in sight of the Scots border on July 7, 1307. His son Edward II took over the throne.

The Troubled Reign of Edward II

Edward II's 20-year reign was one that was marked by hardship and failure. The country experienced widespread famine due to repeated bouts of severe weather and poor harvests. Additionally, England's military accomplishments suffered in France and Scotland.

Edward's greatest failure, however, came in the political arena, where he favored two men, Piers Gaveston and Hugh le Despenser. The nature of Edward's relationships with these men is unknown, but some historians believe they may have been romantic. Edward showered Gaveston with lavish gifts and property even before he had become king. That ended when a group of nobles, offended by the relationship, forced the king to exile Gaveston. Gaveston eventually returned to England, but he was then arrested and executed for treason.

The king repeated this behavior with Despenser. By 1324, Edward's wife, Isabella of France, had had enough. Her brother ruled France, and, pretending she wanted to meet with him to mend English relations with France, Isabella sailed to Europe. There she began a relationship with Roger Mortimer, a leading member of the group that opposed Despenser. Her eldest son, Edward III, joined her, and in September 1326, she, her son, and Mortimer led an army to England. Popular support for the king quickly faded away. The king was arrested in November, and on January 20, 1327, the lords in Parliament sentenced him to life in prison. Four days later he abdicated, or gave up, the throne to his son. Edward II was later executed, possibly on the orders of Isabella or Mortimer.

A Reign Modeled on King Arthur

After his father abdicated, 14-year-old Edward III embarked on a 50-year reign. His leadership abilities led to a period of rare internal peace with the English nobles, and he also oversaw historically significant military victories in Scotland and France.

Edward first led English forces against Scotland in 1327. His army's skill with a new weapon, the longbow, brought him an overwhelming victory at Halidon Hill in 1333, during the Second War of Scottish Independence. He also became involved in a succession crisis in France when its king, Charles IV, who was Edward's uncle, died without a male heir in 1328. Although Edward believed he had a legitimate claim to the crown, he bided his time for several years. He encouraged hostility toward the French among his people and his nobles, and in 1337, he began a series of campaigns that opened what is now called the Hundred Years' War. In 1346, his most important victory of that war came at Crécy, in northern France, where once again, his longbowmen were the key to winning the battle.

Edward's success in raising money and men for these expensive campaigns was due to his excellent relations with his nobles. His court was modeled on the mythical King Arthur's Knights of the Round Table, in which chivalry and cooperation were the most important qualities. Edward invited Europe's greatest knights to his court to test their strength and courage at his tournaments, which spread England's prestige far and wide.

Starting in 1360, however, Edward III's reign steadily declined. He had lost a daughter and one of his sons to the bubonic plague, a deadly disease that is often referred to as the Black Death. Historians estimate that the plague killed nearly 2 million people between 1348 and 1350; many crops and animals also died because of a lack of people to tend them. With scarce food supplies, famine and poverty spread. Europe was socially and economically unstable, and Edward could not rule effectively under such circumstances. When he died in 1377, the crown passed to his 10-year-old grandson, Richard II.

Despite the uncertainty in postplague Europe, Richard encouraged the development of cultural pursuits, including literature, and it was during his reign that Geoffrey Chaucer wrote *The Canterbury Tales*, which was published between 1387 and 1400. However, Richard's reign was a turbulent 22 years, troubled by revolts over taxation and internal disputes between nobles. His most loyal supporter was his uncle, John of Gaunt, Duke of Lancaster. John was the head of the Lancaster branch of the Plantagenets and the premier lord in England, second in power only to the king. When John of Gaunt died in 1399, his son, Henry Bolingbroke, moved against the king. Henry captured Richard, imprisoned him, and forced him to abdicate. Thus, Bolingbroke was crowned King Henry IV on October 13, 1399.

The House of Lancaster

Henry IV reigned from 1399 to 1413. He was sensitive to threats to his rule; as historian Miri Rubin wrote, "The

Shown here is an illustration of the legendary King Arthur and his Knights of the Round Table.

usurper [someone who takes the throne without the right to it, often by force] was rightly alert to the many possibilities which endangered him; usurpers are open to usurpation, and this became the keynote of Henry IV's reign."[10] In his first few years on the throne, he and his supporters successfully suppressed several challenges and plots against him. He was supported by a core group of allies and by wealth his father had accumulated for the House of Lancaster. As he stabilized the political landscape of England and ended rebellions in Wales, Henry gained more support among his subjects.

Although Henry's place on the throne was secure, he was by no means at peace. Members of Parliament often protested against his demands for funds for his military campaigns. In general, Henry reacted calmly and reasonably to avoid any confrontation that might cost him the throne, but the stress took a toll. He died in March 1413 with his heir apparent, Prince Henry, at his side.

Henry V's reign is one of the most famous in British history. He ruled for just nine years, but during that time, he focused on pressing English claims to the throne of France. He received the support of both Parliament and the people, and he invaded France in August 1415, reigniting the Hundred Years' War. On October 25, his army, outnumbered about three to one, won a stunning victory at Agincourt. Many people, including 4,000 Frenchmen and many nobles, died in the battle, compared with just 400 of Henry's army. Eventually, Henry V was recognized as the next in line to the French throne by the 1420 Treaty of Troyes. He married Catherine of Valois, the daughter of the king of France, and they had a son, also called Henry (He would become Henry VI.), in 1421. However, during the following summer while campaigning in France, Henry V died, therefore never becoming king in France. The French king died shortly after Henry did. When Henry V died, his nine-month-old son was crowned king of England and was also the disputed king of France.

The Nine-Month-Old King
The infant Henry VI was raised by a series of nurses, tutors, and religious educators, as well as trusted household servants from Henry V's staff. His mother, Queen Catherine, lived with her son and helped coordinate his few public appearances before the age of seven, establishing her own household and secretly marrying a Welshman named Owen Tudor. Henry VI's coronation on November 6, 1429, was a formality; a council of men designated in Henry V's will continued to rule England.

The young king declared himself of age in November 1437, just before his 16th birthday. Henry VI was unlike his father, and his rule was not as successful. During his reign, England lost many battles in France and was forced to give up a lot of territory. When the Hundred

Years' War finally ended in 1453 with the French victory at Castillon, the only part of France left in English hands was the northern port town of Calais.

Later that year, the king entered a long period during which he suffered from a debilitating mental illness that is now believed to have been schizophrenia. When he recovered 18 months later, he had no memory of the passage of time. His only son, Edward of Lancaster, was born during this time, but upon his recovery, Henry did not recognize the boy or remember anything about his birth.

During this period and Henry's later recurring periods of mental illness, a struggle for power ensued. Richard Plantagenet, Duke of York, opposed the king's chief advisor, Edmund Beaufort, Duke of Somerset. Richard was the great-grandson of Edward III, so many of his supporters felt that he was entitled to the throne and would make a better king than Henry. Parliament named him Protector of the Realm in 1454, to act in Henry's name until his health improved. This emboldened Richard to imprison Edmund, but when the king recovered in 1455, he freed Edmund and stripped Richard of his title.

Lancaster versus York

Over the next 30 years, intermittent fighting between the allies of Henry VI's House of Lancaster and Richard's House of York undermined peace in England. This conflict between two related branches of the Plantagenet dynasty came to be known as the Wars of the Roses. The name refers to symbols often used by the two houses: Lancaster used red roses; York used white. At its heart, these were feuds between two families and their supporters, with the prize being the throne.

The conflicts began in May 1455 with a battle between the Lancastrians and the Yorkists at St. Albans. The Yorkists won the battle, and Edmund Beaufort was killed. Richard did not try to seize power afterward, however; instead, he regained his position of protector when King Henry's health declined again. In 1456, Henry's queen, Margaret of Anjou, gained the support of his advisors to rule in his place, and Richard was removed for a second time. Margaret despised Richard and encouraged the new Duke of Somerset, Henry Beaufort, to support her and the king as his father had done. Meanwhile, Richard gained the support of Richard Neville, the Earl of Salisbury, and Neville's son Richard, the Earl of Warwick.

In 1459, civil war erupted again. This time, the Lancastrians won at the Battle of Ludlow, but in 1460, the Earl of Warwick returned and defeated the Lancastrians, enabling the Duke of York to press his claim to the throne before Parliament. The Act of Accord recognized the Duke of York as Henry's heir apparent. Henry's queen, Margaret, understandably objected to the settlement as it disinherited her son. She gathered an army of supporters in the north and defeated the Yorkists in

December 1460; both the Duke of York and Earl of Salisbury were killed. Margaret then marched south to London, defeated the Earl of Warwick at the Second Battle of St. Albans, and liberated the king from Yorkist London. The Earl of Warwick, along with the Duke of York's son Edward, retook London three months later in March 1461, and Edward declared himself king. Henry and Margaret fled north, pursued by Edward and the Earl of Warwick; the two armies clashed at Towton, a village in the northern county of Yorkshire, on March 29, 1461, in the middle of a snowstorm. The Lancastrians were defeated, and Henry and Margaret sought refuge in Scotland.

Edward and the Earl of Warwick

Following the Yorkist victory at Towton, Edward of York began his reign as Edward IV. The deposed queen, meanwhile, tried and failed to have Henry returned to the throne. After three years, however, Henry sneaked back into England, hoping to raise an army. He spent a year hiding in the north until he was caught by Edward's supporters in July 1465 and imprisoned in the Tower of London.

During Henry's exile, Edward became a levelheaded ruler and an able administrator. He encouraged English merchants to trade overseas, generating income and prosperity for his nation. The end of war with France meant an end to expensive military campaigns, and taxes were reduced or eliminated, which increased Edward's popularity.

Edward, however, made a significant mistake by antagonizing the Earl of Warwick. For supporting Edward, the earl had been rewarded with the post of chamberlain of England, becoming the second-most powerful man in the land. He negotiated a political marriage between the king and a French princess, only to discover that Edward had already secretly married a commoner, Elizabeth Woodville. The king had been able to keep the marriage secret for four months; when it became public in September 1464, there was a tremendous public uproar. Not only was this marriage seen as unsuitable because Elizabeth was far below the king in social standing and had no royal blood, but her family had also supported the Lancastrians.

The Earl of Warwick was upset, but he stayed loyal, proposing a variety of marriage contracts between the king's family and his own. Edward rejected them all, and when the king arranged for his sister to marry the Duke of Burgundy instead of into the Earl of Warwick's family, the earl broke with Edward. He gave his support to Edward's brother George, Duke of Clarence, who wanted to be king. He then supported a series of rebellions in northern England in 1468, which resulted in Edward's capture in July. The Earl of Warwick imprisoned the king and tried to rule in his name, but he had no support in Parliament to keep the king imprisoned. He released Edward in October 1469, and the king returned to power with much public acclaim.

Complex Politics

To regain his former power, the Earl of Warwick formed an alliance with Margaret of Anjou, the queen of the imprisoned Henry VI. She was still advocating the Lancastrian cause with the support of King Louis XI of France. Louis gave the Earl of Warwick and Margaret an army and a fleet of ships, and they invaded England in September 1470. Edward fled to France, and on October 3, 1470, a puzzled and disheveled Henry was restored to the throne. The Earl of Warwick begged the king's forgiveness.

Henry's return to the throne, however, was short-lived. Edward gained an army from his brother-in-law, the Duke of Burgundy, landed in England in March 1471, and outmaneuvered the Earl of Warwick to enter London in April. Two days later, Henry and the Earl of Warwick fled the capital. Edward's forces caught up with them, the earl was killed, and Henry was imprisoned once more. Margaret returned from France with an invasion force in May, but her army was defeated and her son Edward was killed. The former queen was imprisoned. Edward spared her life but had Henry executed on

THE KINGMAKER

In 1521, John Major became the first historian to describe Richard Neville, Earl of Warwick, as "the kingmaker." It was a fitting name for someone who, in just a few years, removed Henry VI from power, brought Edward IV to the throne, and then oversaw Henry's return.

Such actions made Neville a controversial figure. Historians who were sympathetic to the Yorkist cause depicted him as a great man who was popular in the nation but who was forced to take extreme actions by the betrayal of his friend King Edward. Others were less generous. As early as 1471, the year he was killed at the Battle of Barnet, a character study portrayed Neville as a man driven by ego and a desire for power. Since then, historians have combined these two views—of a power-hungry yet loyal man—into a more balanced depiction of Neville and his motives.

May 21, 1471.

The last dozen years of Edward IV's reign were anticlimactic; when he died on April 9, 1483, the throne passed to his 12-year-old son, Edward V. In his will, the king had named his brother, Richard of Gloucester, as protector until Edward V was old enough to rule independently.

Richard Neville, the Earl of Warwick, is depicted here at the Battle of Barnet, where he was killed.

The House of York Falls

Richard III professed loyalty to the young king; however, this was a lie. In truth, he wanted the throne for himself. Edward V and his younger brother Richard were soon imprisoned in the Tower of London. Richard III then had Edward IV's marriage to Elizabeth Woodville declared invalid, meaning that any children from the marriage (Edward V and Richard) were therefore illegitimate and could not take the throne. These strategic moves put Richard III next in line for the throne. He was named king in June 1483.

However, this kingship did not last long. Because Elizabeth was afraid she would never see her sons again, she entered into an alliance with Henry Tudor, stating he could marry her daughter, also named Elizabeth, if he would support her against Richard III. Henry was the last surviving Lancastrian and the grandson

THE PRINCES IN THE TOWER

During Richard III's quest for the throne in 1483, he succeeded in removing Edward IV's two young sons, the heir apparent Edward (aged 12) and Prince Richard (aged 9), from public view by moving them to live in the Tower of London. The king's nephews were seen playing in the tower grounds occasionally during the summer of 1483, but then the sightings stopped. The princes were never seen in public again.

The mystery surrounding their fates is tied to Richard's ambition for the throne, since the princes' survival would have threatened Richard's ability to take power. Some historians believe that the boys were murdered, possibly on their uncle's orders. In 1674, workers rebuilding part of the tower came across a wooden box with two skeletons inside, thought to be those of the princes. The remains were buried again in Westminster Abbey. In 1933, the bones were examined by leading British forensic experts, who agreed that they belonged to two young males, approximately 13 and 11 years old. However, it is not 100 percent proven that the bones are those of the princes.

In 2018, geneticists obtained a DNA sample from a direct descendant of the princes' maternal grandmother. If the boys' bones from Westminster Abbey were to be tested and matched this DNA, it would show that Richard likely murdered his nephews. However, tests are unlikely to be carried out in the foreseeable future. When the bones were found and examined in the 1930s, it was long before DNA testing was invented, and no genetic material would have been collected and stored for future examination. Additionally, the Abbey is considered a royal peculiar, which means it is a religious institution that is under the authority of the Crown. The Crown will not allow the bones to be unburied again, at least at this time, so the fate of the princes in the tower remains one of British history's greatest mysteries.

This painting depicts Edward and Richard, the princes in the tower.

of Henry V's widow, Catherine of Valois, and Owen Tudor. Henry assembled an army and met Richard's army in Leicestershire. Richard was so intent on killing Henry that he went into battle himself and was killed. Richard had no legitimate son to ascend to the throne, and therefore, Henry Tudor was named king of England, thus claiming the throne through military conquest. With his marriage to Elizabeth, the Wars of the Roses were brought to an end. Henry became king in August 1485, and the House of Tudor began its reign.

CHAPTER THREE

THE TUDORS

Henry Tudor's claim to the throne was not as strong as Richard III's had been, but his crowning nonetheless marked the start of a new dynasty. Henry Tudor—now Henry VII—had a successful reign but was never able to fully enjoy his triumphs because of the personal tragedies he experienced in his life.

Henry VII: The First Tudor King

Henry VII soon received support from Parliament and the Catholic Church. In November 1485, Parliament met in London to proclaim him the legitimate king of England. The following January, Pope Innocent VIII declared Henry the rightful ruler of the land and threatened anyone who opposed him with excommunication from the Church. Despite this support, his rule was still challenged. Some of his opponents were executed or imprisoned, but others were pardoned.

Henry succeeded in establishing good will with other nations and ushered in a period of domestic calm in England—something that had been a rarity for many years. He forged a peace treaty with Scotland in 1502; his daughter Margaret married the Scots king James IV the following year. He also agreed to a marriage between his first son, Arthur, and Catherine of Aragon when the boy was a toddler. Catherine was the daughter of the king and queen of Spain, and the agreement helped foster mutual good will between England and one of the richest nations in Europe. Arthur and Catherine married in 1501, when Arthur was 15.

England's finances were also improving. Henry kept tight control over government spending, and the economy flourished as the threat of further civil war receded. However, Henry was not at peace personally. His son Arthur died in 1502 at age 15, just six months after his marriage to

Catherine, and Henry's wife, Elizabeth, died in 1503 shortly after giving birth. Henry died in 1509 at 52. As Mike Ashley wrote, "Personally Henry was a sad king ... perhaps never truly enjoying the success that he achieved."[11]

Henry VIII

When Henry VII died, his second son, Henry VIII, became king. The now teenaged Henry VIII had become the heir apparent when his older brother Arthur had died in 1502, and he was two months shy of his 18th birthday when his father died. The dying king wished for Henry to marry Arthur's widow, Catherine of Aragon, in order to continue the alliance with Spain. The wedding took place six weeks after Henry VII's death.

Henry VIII's personality differed from his father's. He was outgoing whereas his father was reserved, and as a young prince, he had enjoyed touring the land and meeting with the people. He was a natural athlete, a fine horseman, and an accomplished linguist, musician, and composer. However, these skills and achievements are not why he remains one of England's most famous kings. Instead, he is most often remembered for the decisions he made in his personal life—ones that eventually redefined the roles of religion and royalty in England.

Anne Boleyn

For the first few years of Henry's reign, his marriage to his brother's widow, Catherine of Aragon, seemed peaceful, if somewhat unhappy. They had a daughter, Mary, in 1516, but there were also five other children who did not survive. After 10 years of marriage, Henry believed that Catherine was incapable of having a son. Additionally, he became convinced that God was cursing him for marrying his brother's wife, and he began to seek a divorce. Divorce was highly uncommon and prohibited by the Catholic Church, but Henry insisted. The issue, known as Henry's "great matter," rocked the entire nation.

Henry and his counselors tried to convince Pope Clement VII that the marriage should be dissolved, but Clement resisted. The matter dragged on for years, and it was complicated by the appearance of Anne Boleyn at Henry's court. Anne was a lady-in-waiting to Catherine of Aragon, and she was admired at court as an attractive woman with sophisticated manners. Henry previously had had an affair with Anne's sister, Mary, and then pursued Anne relentlessly because he had grown tired of his wife and their inability to have a male heir. However, Anne rejected Henry's advances. Just before Christmas 1526, after 18 months of pursuing her, Henry said to Anne in a letter, "I promise ... to take you as my sole mistress, casting off all others than yourself out of mind and affection and to serve you and you alone."[12] However, Anne had no wish to be the king's mistress—she wanted to be queen.

As the papal court refused to resolve

More than 500 years later, Henry VIII remains one of England's most memorable kings.

Henry VIII pursued Anne Boleyn for more than a year but had her beheaded three years after marrying her.

the "great matter"—the divorce from one woman in order to marry another who might bear him an heir—in Henry's favor, both he and his ministers began to feel that the only way he could end his marriage with Catherine was to take matters into his own hands.

Henry had been a loyal Catholic his entire life. For example, when protesters in Europe began to clamor for reforms to many of the Church's practices, such as the sale of indulgences (the ability to have sins forgiven in exhange for payments to the Church), Henry had defended the Church. However, this movement, which came to be called the Protestant Reformation, was gaining momentum across Europe, and with it, Henry recognized an opportunity to resolve his problem. He persuaded Parliament to declare that he—not the pope—was the supreme head of the Church in England. With that move, the king and government officially broke from the Catholic Church and established the Church of England. The proclamation enabled Henry to grant his own divorce. Catherine was banished from court and lived in Cambridgeshire until her death in 1536.

Henry and Anne Boleyn were married in a secret ceremony in January 1533, and she was crowned queen the following spring. When she became pregnant, she and the king were convinced that she would have a son, but the healthy child, born on September 7, 1533, was a girl. They named her Elizabeth. The couple believed that a son would follow, but two additional children, including a boy, died at birth. Henry's sadness over not having a son deepened, and he began to believe rumors that Anne had been unfaithful to him—an accusation which may or may not be true—and that she practiced witchcraft. Based on these accusations, Henry VIII imprisoned Anne in the Tower of London. On May 15, 1536, she was given a trial, during which she calmly denied all charges against her. However, the jury found her guilty, and she was beheaded on May 19, 1536.

Jane, Anne, and Catherine

Next, Henry fell for Jane Seymour, the daughter of one of his knights. Jane was shy and reserved instead of outspoken as Anne had been, but she, too, wished to be Henry's wife and not his mistress. They were married just 11 days after Anne's execution, and she was proclaimed queen in June. On October 12, 1537, Jane gave birth to a healthy boy whom the couple named Edward. However, Jane fell ill two days after his birth and died 10 days later. Henry was devastated by her death, but he now had the male heir he had so desperately wanted.

The king remained without a queen for more than two years until he agreed to a political marriage that would strengthen his ties to Protestant rulers in Germany. He agreed to a marriage to Anne of Cleves after seeing her picture. However, when Anne arrived in

England in January 1540 and Henry met her in person, he no longer thought she was attractive. The marriage went ahead anyway but lasted only seven months before both agreed to an annulment.

Henry's next choice for a wife—now his fifth—was Catherine Howard. However, Catherine soon tired of her husband, and when he discovered she was not faithful to him, he had her beheaded in the Tower of London on February 13, 1542.

The Sixth Wife of Henry VIII

Catherine Parr, at 33, was unlike any of Henry VIII's previous wives, as she was already twice-widowed when she married Henry in 1543. Henry's children liked their new stepmother, and she helped direct their education for several years and succeeded in re-uniting them with their father. Mary, still a devout Catholic, and Elizabeth, increasingly Protestant, had been declared illegitimate when Edward was born, but Henry returned them to the inheritance in his later years.

By this time, Henry was ill and knew that his days were coming to a close. In his will, he directed that a council of advisors should act as regents for his heir, nine-year-old Edward. Henry died on January 28, 1547, at age 55.

Henry VIII left behind a complicated legacy. Breaking with the Catholic Church stripped the clergy of much of its wealth and power, but thousands of Henry's subjects refused to desert the Church. It had been the foundation of their lives for generations, longer than the practice of showing allegiance to the king. Henry's actions served him well, as it enriched his treasury and enabled him to change wives at will, but it also divided his people between those who were devoted to the original Church and those who were bent on driving it out. Although Henry skillfully negotiated a series of alliances with European powers, his turbulent personal life nearly ruined his ability to have a son succeed him to the throne. According to historians John Cannon and Ralph Griffiths, "If the primary objective of Henry's policy was to secure the succession, he could hardly have done worse. Six marriages had produced one sickly son, and two princesses, whose inheritance had been placed in jeopardy"[13] by Henry's changing whims.

Henry's actions seem arbitrary and cruel, but one reason for his erratic behavior may have been genetic. In 2011, researchers Catarina Whitley and Kyra Kramer suggested that Henry VIII may have had a genetic disease called McLeod syndrome. It generally sets in around age 40, with physical symptoms that include heart disease, muscle weakness, and fatigue, and psychological symptoms such as paranoia. Whitley and Kramer suggested the syndrome could explain the king's behavioral changes in his later years. "This gives us an alternative way of interpreting Henry and understanding his life," Whitley said. "It gives us a new way to look at the reasons he changed."[14]

Lady Jane Grey

With Henry's death, the young Edward VI came to the throne. However, his uncle, Edward Seymour, the Duke of Somerset, usurped the late king's plans for a council of regents when he seized power and became the Protector of the Realm. He was overthrown in 1549 by John Dudley, who became the Duke of Northumberland. Under their influence, Edward directed further Protestant reforms, including the Acts of Uniformity of 1549 and 1552, which standardized Church of England services. For example, masses conducted in Latin were eliminated in favor of worship directed by the English-language Book of Common Prayer.

These initiatives depended on the support of the Protestant king. Edward's hope for a Protestant England extended to his will, in which he directed that his Catholic half sister, Mary, should be passed over in favor of his Protestant cousin Lady Jane Grey, the granddaughter of Henry VIII's youngest sister.

Early in 1553, Edward fell ill with what was most likely tuberculosis, and although at first doctors believed he would recover, he suffered a relapse and died on July 6, 1553, at 15 years old. Three days later, on July 9, the late king's circle of advisors, known as the Privy Council, offered the throne to Lady Jane Grey. The 15-year-old was reluctant to accept, but she did so in order to continue the Protestant reforms. She was proclaimed queen the next day. However, the English people showed overwhelming support for Mary, and Jane abdicated after just nine days.

The Reign of Mary I

Mary was crowned the first queen regnant of England on October 1, 1553. As queen regnant, she was a ruling queen with power over the realm although she had not gained her title through marriage to the king. Cannon and Griffiths state that her reign, "which began with so striking a demonstration of loyalty, is the most tragic, publicly and personally, in English history. On the character of Mary, historians differ. What to some is steadfast courage in adversity is to others no more than stubborn bigotry, nor perhaps are the two always far apart."[15]

Mary had been raised a Catholic by her mother and had remained so as the Protestant Reformation swept England. When she became queen, she was 37 and still single. She revoked several of Henry VIII's measures that discriminated against Catholics but felt that returning England completely to the Catholic Church would endanger her rule. She nonetheless sanctioned a campaign of persecution against Protestant reformers, and nearly 300 were burned at the stake between February 1555 and November 1558.

The queen, who had enjoyed such popularity at the start, became known as Bloody Mary.

Mary also lost support when she married Philip of Spain, the heir to the Spanish throne, in 1554. She loved him deeply but was heartbroken when he did not return her love. She was also crushed when, in 1554 and again in 1557, she believed she was pregnant but actually was not. In the fall of 1558, weak and ailing, she acknowledged her half sister Elizabeth as her heir. She died on November 17, 1558, of unknown causes.

Elizabeth I Inherits the Throne

When both Edward and Mary died childless, the 25-year-old Elizabeth inherited the throne. People lit bonfires in celebration and threw parties in the streets to celebrate her ascension.

Elizabeth I reigned for 45 years, a rule that characterized one of England's most triumphant and admirable periods in history. Her reign was successful in political matters, and she

When Elizabeth I inherited the throne, the people celebrated. This painting shows her on an outing accompanied by her courtiers.

rode horseback on "progresses" across the country in which she would tour the regions. Throughout her reign, she went on more than 25 such trips. Additionally, to look the part of a queen, she wore expensive jewelry and clothes that can be seen in paintings of her.

During Elizabeth's reign, the arts thrived. The construction of country houses such as Longleat and Hardwick Hall showed off magnificent architecture, and theater reached new heights of popularity. The playwright William Shakespeare entertained audiences with insightful stories about royalty and common people alike—Elizabeth even saw some of Shakespeare's plays.

Additionally, Edmund Spenser's epic poem *The Faerie Queene* was dedicated to Elizabeth, and the character of Gloriana was a symbol of the queen.

Despite her popularity, Elizabeth understood that, as a woman, she was vulnerable to the ambitions of the powerful men of her realm. For centuries, female members of royalty were used as pawns to cement political alliances both at home and abroad. The new queen recognized that any marriage, no matter how politically advantageous, could lead to jealousy and conspiracy among the English nobles. She also realized that a political marriage was important for producing an heir and strengthening ties in Europe.

The queen had several suitors, but she turned down all offers of marriage.

Hundreds of years after he created famous works such as A Midsummer Night's Dream, *William Shakespeare continues to be one of the most influential figures in the literary world.*

A MYSTERY IN VIRGINIA

One of the iconic stories of the reign of Queen Elizabeth I is the enduring mystery of the "lost colony" of Roanoke Island. On this small island just west of North Carolina's Outer Banks, more than 100 men, women, and children attempted to start a new life in the New World in 1587. Their sponsor, Sir Walter Raleigh, and their governor, John White, had intended to establish the colony on the southern banks of Chesapeake Bay. A variety of circumstances, however, led them to start their new lives at a military camp on Roanoke Island that Raleigh's men had abandoned two years before.

Poor living conditions forced John White to return to England to petition for more supplies, but the threat of war with Spain delayed his return voyage for three years. When he did come back, in 1590, he found the village eerily deserted. Additionally, White found a carving in a post of the word "Croatoan." To this day, no one knows what happened to the people of the colony, which included White's daughter and son-in-law, as well as their child, Virginia Dare. Most people think the people of the colony encountered disease or violence.

This mystery continues to fascinate people. In fact, the TV show *American Horror Story* came up with its own twist on the Roanoke mystery in 2016, with a season titled *American Horror Story: Roanoke*. The mystery of the lost colony is commemorated at the Fort Raleigh National Historic Site in Manteo, North Carolina.

By the time her last serious suitor died in 1584, Elizabeth was more than 50 years old and beyond her childbearing years. Some suggested that, in her choice to stay single, Elizabeth was putting the nation's needs ahead of her own, and in the early years of her reign, one of these needs was to heal the religious divisions that had arisen during Mary's years.

Elizabeth tried to heal this rift by keeping to the middle ground between Protestantism and Catholicism; she did not wish to follow in the steps of her siblings and choose one side over the other. However, Pope Pius V did not agree with how she was ruling. In 1570, he ordered that she be excommunicated from the Church and that England return to Catholicism. This created a rift in her kingdom, and her people felt they could not be loyal to both the Church and the monarchy.

Shown here is a stone marker at the site of the "lost colony" of Roanoke.

As a result, Protestants persecuted Catholics, and Elizabeth lost the delicate balance she had tried to keep between the two religions. Additionally, during this time, Elizabeth also had to deal with her Catholic cousin, Mary.

The Queen of Scots

Mary, Queen of Scots, was a member of Scotland's House of Stuart. Mary was a devout Catholic and, as the granddaughter of Henry VIII's sister, was also Elizabeth's cousin. In 1543, she had been crowned queen of Scotland at nine months old after her father, King James V, died. At five years old, she moved to France in preparation for marrying the future French king Francis II. She returned to Scotland after his death in 1561, but by then, the Scots Parliament had declared that the nation was Protestant. Mary found herself at the center of several plots connected to Catholic persecution and quests for power.

In 1566, Mary married the Englishman Henry Stuart, also known as Lord Darnley, in a Catholic ceremony, and that same year, she gave birth to a son, James, who was baptized a Catholic. Several Protestant Scots leaders opposed Mary and Lord Darnley, and Lord Darnley was assassinated early in 1567. Although Mary later married the Earl of Bothwell, this time in a Protestant ceremony, a group of lords distrusted her conversion to Protestantism. These lords imprisoned Mary, wishing to replace her with her one-year-old son in hopes of controlling the power of the throne. Mary abdicated in July 1567 in favor of her son, who became King James VI. She escaped from prison the following year and fled to England, hoping that Elizabeth would grant her asylum. She hoped to raise an army and return to Scotland. However,

fearing that her cousin would become a focal point for Catholic rebellion in England, Elizabeth placed Mary under house arrest, severely restricting her freedom to go where she wanted, for the next 18 years.

English and Scots Catholics tried to plan rebellions in Mary's name, and in 1586, Mary implicated herself in a plot to assassinate Elizabeth in connection with an invasion from Catholic Spain. She was put on trial for her role in the conspiracy and found guilty of treason. Elizabeth reluctantly signed her cousin's death warrant, and Mary, Queen of Scots, was beheaded on February 8, 1587. Elizabeth then bestowed a pension on Mary's son James, effectively recognizing him as her heir.

In March 1603, Elizabeth I died, and her advisors sent a message to James VI of Scotland, ending the reign of the Tudors and beginning the reign of the Stuarts.

Chapter Four

THE AGE OF THE STUARTS

Upon hearing of the death of Elizabeth I, James VI left quickly for England to assume the role of king. In July 1603, he was crowned King James I of England, but he was unwilling to give up his Scottish title and also remained King James VI of Scotland. When he took the throne in England, he was only partially prepared for the struggles that awaited him during his 22-year reign.

James I

James I was soon challenged by English traditions and methods of government. The Scots Parliament had only one chamber, made up of nobles who inherited their positions. The English Parliament, on the other hand, had two: the House of Lords, which was occupied by nobles, and the House of Commons, made up of elected, untitled men. The Scots Parliament had generally followed the king's will without objections; the English Parliament regularly debated

and rejected his proposals. For example, in March 1604, James I proposed uniting the two kingdoms of England and Scotland under the name of Great Britain. The Scots Parliament approved the idea; the English Parliament rejected it. While James called himself the king of Great Britain, the two nations continued to have separate governments. The new king was also uncomfortable with petitioning the House of Commons for various expenditures. Consequently, James "dissolved" Parliament several times during his reign when its members refused to do his bidding. The members were dismissed and prevented from being involved in state matters until the king recalled them, often because he needed money.

James's reign was marked by several political successes outside of Parliament, however. Since he was king of both England and Scotland, the cross-border wars between the two nations ended. He also succeeded in ending the conflict with Spain, even as he challenged Spain's global influence by encouraging English expansion into the New World. During his reign, permanent colonies were established on the island of Bermuda, at Jamestown (named in his honor and located in present-day Virginia), and at Plymouth (in present-day Massachusetts). He also succeeded in negotiating international alliances with European Protestant leaders through arranged marriages; his most successful was the marriage of his daughter Elizabeth to Frederick, the elector of Palatine. (Palatine was an electorate, or state, of the Holy Roman Empire in what is now Germany.)

Among European monarchs, James also was a leading supporter of the divine right of kings, which was the belief that God chose kings to rule, and thus kings only had to answer to God, rather than to other men. However, James is most remembered for his translation and adaptation of the Bible into what has become known as the King James Version, which was published in 1611.

Running both kingdoms took its toll on James. His elder son, Henry, the Prince of Wales, died in 1612, making James's younger son, Charles, the heir apparent. Before James died on March 27, 1625, he warned Charles about the growing power of Parliament and the dangers that awaited his son as king. Charles, however, failed to listen to the advice.

Chosen by God

Charles I believed, as his father had, that he had been chosen by God to be king, and as a result, he did not recognize any earthly authority over his command. This attitude got him into trouble throughout his reign.

During his first three years on the throne, Charles found himself at war, first with Spain and then with France, due in large part to military aggressions by the Duke of Buckingham. The duke, who had been a close friend and advisor to James I, continued under Charles to mount ill-advised and expensive military campaigns that resulted in English defeats. Each one led Charles to petition Parliament for more money, and like his father, he discovered that Parliament often rejected him, mainly because the Duke of Buckingham was unpopular.

The duke's assassination in 1628 did not improve Charles's relations with Parliament. Instead, Charles became increasingly influenced by his French Catholic wife, Henrietta Maria, rather than his Protestant advisors. He continued to demand more money and refused to listen to opposing opinions. Frustrated by the fights with Parliament and convinced that he was chosen by God to be king, Charles dismissed Parliament in March 1629 and ruled without it for the next decade.

Old and New Animosities

When Charles finally did call a new Parliament in April 1639, the old

GUY FAWKES DAY

On the evening of November 5, 1605, a former soldier named Guy Fawkes was discovered in the basement beneath the hall where Parliament was scheduled to open the next day. Nearby was a pile of firewood that hid 30 barrels of gunpowder. Fawkes had a pocket watch and matches in his possession and was immediately taken into custody. His arrest led to the discovery of the so-called Gunpowder Plot against King James I and the members of Parliament.

As authorities rounded up Fawkes's colleagues, the details of the conspiracy came to light. The men had planned to blow up the gunpowder to assassinate the king and other members of the government when Parliament opened and thus spark a Catholic uprising in England. The conspirators then intended to place the king's Catholic daughter, Elizabeth, on the throne.

Two of Fawkes's coconspirators were killed while resisting arrest; Fawkes and three others were interrogated, tried, and executed for treason. The plot was the work of only a small group of extremists, but the persecution of Catholics intensified afterward. Citizens were encouraged to light bonfires to celebrate the king's escape, a practice that continues in England every November 5, as bonfires and fireworks mark Guy Fawkes Day. Fawkes continues to be a symbol of protest even outside of England. Members of the hacktivist group called Anonymous hide their identities behind masks designed to look like Fawkes's face.

Protesters who wish to disguise themselves sometimes wear masks with a stylized version of Guy Fawkes's face.

animosities had not disappeared. On the contrary, they were accompanied by new ones. Charles had been trying to impose Church of England standards on the Scots church to make worshipping the same throughout the kingdom. The Scots objected, and Charles tried to enforce his policy by force, only to suffer a humiliating defeat. At the same time, an offshoot of Protestantism called Puritanism was gaining followers throughout the country. Puritans believed in a strict interpretation of the Bible and severe restrictions on dress and behavior. The new Parliament, which included many Puritans, refused to finance an additional military campaign, and in response, the king dismissed this Parliament after just a few weeks. The following year, the pattern was repeated, except that this time, the leaders of Parliament agreed to consider the king's funding request if he would listen to their grievances and not dismiss them. This session became known as the Long Parliament.

By January 1642, however, Charles had tired of Parliament's endless demands for civil reform and tax relief, and he tried to have his opponents arrested. The plan failed, and Charles realized too late that he had gone too far. He fled London to try to rally support for his cause but had no success. In August 1642, Charles declared war on the opposition.

Those who supported the king in the war that followed were called Royalists or Cavaliers. The Parliamentarians were called Roundheads, after the shape of the helmets they wore. The Cavaliers won the early battles, but the Roundheads' New Model Army, led by Sir Thomas Fairfax and Oliver Cromwell, achieved important victories at Marston Moor in 1644 and at Naseby in 1645. After his defeat at Naseby, Charles sought refuge in Scotland but was handed over to Fairfax and Cromwell, who tried to get him to agree to a written constitution. He escaped their custody and fled to Scotland again, where he raised an army, but he was defeated in August 1648.

The Roundheads' leaders insisted that the king be put on trial for waging war against his people, and the House of Commons convened a court of justice in January 1649. Charles, a lifelong believer in the divine right of kings, refused to recognize that the court had authority over him and offered no arguments in his defense. By a one-vote margin, the court condemned him to death on January 27, 1649. The Parliamentarians had killed the king; now, the challenge was to run the nation without one.

The Civil War

The conflict between the Royalists and the Parliamentarians is known in British history as the Civil War. As Mike Ashley wrote, "This was not the first civil war to divide England, and it was not the first to result in the deposition of a king, but because it was the first and only war to result in the abolition of the

Charles I's belief that he was chosen by God and could do no wrong eventually led to his execution.

kingship, it has become known as the Civil War."[16] Parliament quickly abolished the House of Lords for its support of the king, leaving only the House of Commons. This body, known as the Rump Parliament, then passed a law forbidding anyone from proclaiming another king. Instead, the leadership of the new republic, which was called the Commonwealth of England, fell to Oliver Cromwell.

Cromwell had been a member of Parliament since 1628, and as the leader of the victorious Roundheads, he seemed to be the best choice for building a bridge between the army and Parliament. Following the king's execution, Cromwell returned to Parliament and was selected to serve on the Council of State, the new executive body of Parliament created to help run England. However, additional military campaigns distracted him from diplomatic matters. He and his army were dispatched to stop an uprising of Catholics and Royalists in Ireland. His nine-month campaign there led to widespread destruction and deportations of Irish rebels to English colonies in America. He then went to Scotland to deal with a similar rebellion, where Royalists had named the late king's son, Charles Stuart, King Charles II.

By 1652, the rebellions had been defeated, and Stuart was in exile in Europe. Cromwell returned to Parliament, but in 1653, he accused it of refusing to move forward with elections and reforms and dissolved it with the help of his army. The following year, he was sworn in as Lord Protector under a new government framework. The position was his for life.

For the next six years, Cromwell ruled in much the same way as previous kings had. Before he died on September 3, 1658, he designated his son as his successor. His son's brief time as Lord Protector was highly ineffective, and by 1660, there was a popular movement to restore the monarchy. From exile in Holland, Charles Stuart returned to England on May 25, 1660, and was crowned Charles II the following April. The Commonwealth was no more.

The Return of the Monarchy

With the return of the monarchy, called the Restoration, a newly elected Parliament rolled back many of the reforms instituted during the Commonwealth, such as the bans on many public celebrations and feast days. People liked the new king, who inspired a rebirth of the arts and sciences through his participation in many activities that the Puritans had forbidden. Charles II not only lifted the Puritan ban on theater but regularly attended performances throughout London. He established the Royal Society in 1660 to expand scientific investigation of the natural world and lent support to the Royal Observatory to study astronomy.

An underlying current of religious intolerance remained, however. Each subsequent election sent more Puritans to Parliament, and laws passed to ban minority faiths troubled the king. Although not formally a member of the Catholic Church, he had developed Catholic tendencies during his years in exile, and he married Catherine of Braganza, a Portuguese Catholic, in 1662. His brother James, the Duke of York, was openly Catholic. Suspicions of the king's true sympathies increased when he issued his Royal Declaration of Indulgence in 1672, which allowed private worship for Catholics and suspended penalties for those who did not follow the Protestant ways of the Church of England.

In 1683, the so-called Rye House Plot was a plan formed by some of the king's opponents and his illegitimate son to assassinate both Charles and James. The goal of the plot was to put the king's illegitimate son on the throne. When the king and his supporters discovered the plot, they ordered the executions of many who were involved in it.

After the Rye House incident, Charles's reign was peaceful. He did not live much longer, however, as he suffered a stroke and died on February 6, 1685, at age 54. He and his wife had no legitimate children, so the throne passed to his brother James, now James II.

James II

Because of James II's strong Catholic faith, suspicions arose that England was heading toward rejoining the Catholic Church and undoing the work of Henry VIII. To many Protestants and a large number of members of Parliament, this was unacceptable. Their hopes for a continued Protestant England lay in James's daughters from his first wife, both of whom were Protestants. His daughter Mary had married William III of Orange, one of the leading Protestants in Holland, and Anne had married George, the brother of the king of Denmark, a Protestant country. The belief was that because James and his second wife were childless, upon his death, the throne would pass to Mary. However, in the summer of 1688, James's wife gave birth to a healthy son named James Francis Edward Stuart.

On June 30, 1688, the bishop of London and six supporters wrote to William of Orange, inviting him to England to take over the government. They assured him that many citizens desired change and hoped that he would protect his wife's claim to the throne. William agreed, and in November, he landed with an army in southwestern England. Mary supported William's invasion against her father, believing it was her religious duty to support her husband.

James lost his support in the government, and his daughter Anne abandoned him as well. In December, James fled from London, and William accepted the reins of government. The following year, a member of Parliament described the events as a "Glorious

Revolution," the name by which it is still known today.

William III and Mary II

When Parliament met in early 1689, its members declared that James had abdicated by deserting the country, which cleared the way for Mary to become queen. Mary, however, was uncomfortable being the sole ruler as it might appear that she had usurped her father's throne. William, for his part, did not want to be a prince consort. A series of negotiations resulted in Parliament offering William and Mary joint sovereignty. In other words, they would rule equally, and one would continue to rule if the other died.

Before they were offered the crown, William and Mary were asked to agree to a number of resolutions called the Declaration of Right. The declaration limited the sovereign's power, reaffirmed Parliament's right to tax and legislate, required the sovereign to call an assembly of Parliament frequently, and dictated that the sovereign affirm the Protestant faith in the coronation speech. It further excluded James II and his heirs from the throne—as well as all Catholics—since "it hath been found by experience that it is inconsistent with the safety and welfare of this protestant kingdom to be governed by a papist prince."[17] Following their acceptance of the declaration, the husband and wife were crowned William III and Mary II on April 11, 1689.

After the Declaration of Right, Parliament passed additional measures that limited the power of the monarchy. One act required the monarch to call for Parliamentary elections at least every three years, and another prohibited funding a standing army in peacetime unless given permission by the Commons. Each of these contributed to the formation of England's constitutional monarchy, in which the sovereign remains the head of the nation, but the power over day-to-day affairs and to make laws lies in Parliament.

The Act of Succession

The partnership under which William and Mary governed changed when Mary contracted smallpox and died in December 1694. Gilbert Burnet, the bishop of Salisbury, wrote that when Mary died, William's "spirits sunk so low that there was great reason to apprehend that he was following her."[18] They had no children, and William never remarried. According to the line of succession, Mary's sister Anne would then take the throne. However, succession laws in place at the time did not provide for a monarch beyond Anne. She had had a son, William, but he died in 1700 at age 11, leaving no direct heirs to the throne after Anne's death and prompting a succession crisis. Additionally, because Anne's half brother, James Francis Edward Stuart, was Catholic, he was barred from ascending to the throne on the basis of his religion.

The challenge was to find and designate an heir who fit both the hereditary

Mary II took over the throne with her husband, William III of Orange.

Queen Anne took the throne in 1702.

KINGDOM OF GREAT BRITAIN

In the early 1700s, both King William III and his successor Queen Anne proposed that the kingdoms of England and Scotland be formally unified. The Scots objected, mostly due to the 1701 Act of Succession. They wanted the freedom to choose their own monarch when Anne died. The English Parliament forced the matter in 1705 when it passed the Aliens Act, which, if enforced, would have treated Scots as foreigners and prohibited trade with Scotland. The Scots eventually accepted the Hanoverian succession, and negotiations led to the Acts of Union passed by each Parliament.

Under the Act, Scotland and England united as "Great Britain." Now, both nations would use the same money and have the same flag. The act also reformed land taxes in Scotland and gave the country economic equality with England. Additionally, the Scots Parliament would be abolished, with Scottish representatives included in a new British Parliament. Both parties agreed to the terms, and on May 1, 1707, the union of the two kingdoms became official, and the Kingdom of Great Britain was born.

and Parliamentary requirements. In 1701, Parliament passed the Act of Succession, which bypassed the Catholic heirs in favor of Princess Sophia, electress of Hanover, Germany. She was the daughter of the queen of Bohemia and a granddaughter of James I. At the time, she was already 70, so it seemed unlikely that she would live to rule in England. However, her son George Louis was 40, and her grandson George Augustus was 17. The act seemed to settle the dynastic question of who would rule after Anne died. William III died in 1702 and Anne, the last of the Protestant Stuarts, ascended to the throne at the age of 37.

Anne was popular among the people. If she believed an advisor or minister did not have the nation's interests in mind, she dismissed them. She was also a loyal supporter of the Church of England and set up a fund, called Queen Anne's Bounty, to help pay poorer clergy members.

Anne died in 1714, shortly after Sophia died. This made Sophia's son George the heir apparent. With the death of Anne, the age of the Stuarts ended, and George became king.

CHAPTER FIVE

THE HANOVERIAN REIGN

Although Parliament had passed the Act of Succession more than a decade before Anne died, it had yet to be put into practice, and many expected that the change in power would not be smooth. In the words of John Cannon and Ralph Griffiths, "Everything pointed to a desperate race for the throne" between George Louis, elector of Hanover, and James II's son James Francis Edward Stuart, who lived in France. Instead it was, according to Cannon and Griffiths, "one of the grand anti-climaxes of British history."[19]

James made no move to assert his claim to the throne, and in October 1714, George Louis was crowned King George I with no fanfare. By this time, according to Mike Ashley, "the power of the king was waning against the growing power of Parliament and, while the authority of the king retained a certain mystical aura, this was not what it had been before the Civil War and the English were already starting to regard the monarch as a figurehead."[20] Nonetheless, George's ascension to the throne began the more than 100-year-long reign of Hanoverian kings.

The First Hanoverian King

George I was well educated and took an interest in a number of scientific pursuits, such as the latest agricultural advancements. He particularly enjoyed music, including the work of composer George Frideric Handel. In fact, Handel composed his widely celebrated *Water Music* for one of the king's parties in 1717. The king also created the first Royal Academy of Music in 1719.

Because George's first language was German, he relied on his son George Augustus, Prince of Wales, to translate for him at cabinet meetings where English was spoken. The relationship between the two was strained, however, and after they had an argument in 1717, the prince stopped going to

George I's coronation marked the start of a century of rule by Hanoverian kings.

cabinet meetings and instead assembled a group of his own advisors from the government, including Robert Walpole, the leader of the majority Whig Party in Parliament. The dispute with his son forced George to find someone else to represent him at the cabinet meetings and to provide direction for the government. Today, this post is known as the prime minister.

In 1720, George I and George Augustus reconciled, which meant Walpole was included in George I's administration. Although the title did not yet exist, some historians consider Walpole Britain's first prime minister. George I did not like Walpole, but the king in his later years grudgingly relied on him, and Walpole proved instrumental in helping rescue the nation's economy from disaster and the government from scandal.

A Growing Empire

In June 1727, George I died and was succeeded by George Augustus, who became George II.

Despite their frequent clashes, George II was like his father in some ways. He treated his son, Frederick, the Prince of Wales, much as he had been treated. Frederick, who was 20 when his father became George II, became a popular figure in London. The king and his wife, Caroline, disapproved of much of their son's behavior, however. When Frederick ran up large gambling debts, his parents refused to pay them off. Frederick died in 1751, before his father, but by then, he had married Princess Augusta of Saxe-Gotha-Altenburg and fathered nine children, which removed the king's younger (and favorite) son from the succession.

George II's popularity among his people had grown as the nation prospered. One contributing factor was Britain's colonial empire in North America, which provided a ready market for British goods and was a source of tremendous amounts of raw materials.

By the time George reached his 70s, his health was declining, and he died in October 1760. Frederick's son George assumed the throne upon the death of his grandfather, becoming George III. He was the first king from the House of Hanover to be born in England. Although he could be stubborn, he also appreciated the value of being flexible and open to change. He delayed his coronation until after his marriage to Charlotte of Mecklenburg-Strelitz in September 1761 so they could have a joint ceremony as king and queen.

One of George III's top priorities was to end the war with France and Spain. The Treaty of Paris in 1763 brought an end to the fighting, but it had been a long and expensive war. The British had been involved in battles from Canada to India and were now hard-pressed to pay for them. Parliament tried to raise revenue through a number of taxes on ordinary items. The Stamp Act of 1765 taxed newspapers and other documents. It was so unpopular

American revolutionaries are shown destroying a statue of King George III in this engraving.

HAMILTON AND GEORGE III

The blockbuster Broadway musical *Hamilton* was created by musician and actor Lin-Manuel Miranda after he read Ron Chernow's biography of Alexander Hamilton. Hamilton was involved in the American Revolution and became one of America's Founding Fathers. The musical, which uses hip-hop and rap music, is significant because it tells the story of the American Revolution through a racially diverse cast, representing people whose voices have largely been left out of this history.

Throughout the musical, the character of King George III appears to express his frustration with the Americans. His song "You'll Be Back" incorrectly predicts that the unhappy colonists will eventually remember that they actually belong to the monarchy. As Ben Brantley wrote in the *New York Times*, George "sings an entirely different tune as he observes, from across the Atlantic, that his colonial subjects are revolting, in all senses of the word."[1]

In 2018, Prince Harry and Meghan Markle saw a performance of *Hamilton* in London at the Victoria Palace Theatre. After the show, they went onstage to thank the audience and Harry sang a line from "You'll Be Back." This particular show was a charity performance for Sentebale, a charity Harry established in 2006 to fight HIV. The show was also significant because Prince Harry is a direct descendant of George III—he is George's sixth-great grandson.

1. Ben Brantley, "Review: 'Hamilton,' Young Rebels Changing History and Theater," *New York Times*, August 6, 2015. www.nytimes.com/2015/08/07/theater/review-hamilton-young-rebels-changing-history-and-theater.html.

that it was repealed a year later. The taxes were also unpopular in Britain's colonies, especially in America. People who lived in the colonies had no representation in Parliament, and many believed the government was taxing them without their approval. By 1775, the American colonies were rising up in open rebellion.

Losing the Colonies

At first, George had no intention of letting the colonies leave the empire. His prime minister, Lord North, worked to put down the insurrection, but the war, now known as the American Revolution, dragged on, draining the British treasury. France and Spain helped the Americans, leading to a series of

Hamilton *debuted in 2015, and in 2018, Meghan Markle and Prince Harry met with members of its talented and diverse cast in London.*

stunning victories for the colonists and the surrender of the British army at Yorktown in 1781. Lord North had to accept the fact that the Americans had won. After two years of negotiations, the two sides agreed to the Treaty of Paris in 1783, which recognized American independence.

For a king to lose colonies to another monarch was unfortunate; to grant them independence was humiliating. Rulers were accustomed to succeeding at stopping rebellions, no matter the cost. However, George had come to the realization that American independence was best for all. When he met with the United States ambassador, John Adams, in 1785, the king said, "I will be free with you. I was the last to consent to the separation; but the separation having been made and having become inevitable, I have always said, as I say now, that I would be the first to meet the friendship of the United States as an independent power."[21]

While the British government's reputation suffered tremendously by losing the American colonies, George III remained personally popular among the people. They did not hold him responsible for the hard times that marked the end of the 18th century. Most of the population's complaints, according to Ashley, were "aimed at the government and not directly at George … In fact he was often viewed, especially by the middle classes, as their champion against the government."[22] Despite the loss of the American colonies, it was during George III's reign that Ireland joined Great Britain, creating the United Kingdom of Great Britain and Ireland in 1801.

In 1765, George suffered the first bout of what seemed to be a type of insanity. He talked incessantly or not at all, failed to recognize family members, and acted irrationally and occasionally violently. He recovered but had a second and more severe attack in 1788. By this time, his children were mostly grown and his son George, the Prince of Wales, sought to be declared regent over his father. The king improved once more, however, and the regency was delayed. George III had incidents of his mental illness for the next several years,

however, and the prince eventually was declared regent in 1811. From then until his father's death in 1820, he acted as king in most respects, although he did not hold the title.

Reign of King George IV

George III's son had been a difficult and spoiled child. After several romantic relationships, the prince had married Princess Caroline of Brunswick-Lüneburg (in the German lands of the Holy Roman Empire) in April 1795 at the king's insistence. They had a daughter, Charlotte, but the couple soon discovered they were not well matched. They separated and led lives independent of each other from then on. Charlotte died in 1817 from complications in childbirth, leaving the prince regent without an heir. Caroline, who had been on a European tour when George III died in 1820, returned to England despite her estranged husband's attempts to pay her to stay away. She was not crowned queen at his coronation, and she died 19 days later.

With the ceremony, George became King George IV, officially ending his days as regent. The periods both before and after his coronation, however, are known as the Regency and were marked by extravagance in architecture, fashion, the arts, and entertainment. The king oversaw the massive reconstructions of Windsor Castle in Berkshire and Buckingham Palace in London, and he supported rebuilding a portion of central London into a new park and neighborhood now called the Regent's Park.

The last few years of his reign found George IV in seclusion at Windsor Castle. Politics had never been his strong suit; now, he removed himself from the nation's business altogether. He died on June 26, 1830, at age 67. He left no direct heirs, and the crown passed to his younger brother William, the Duke of Clarence.

Silly Billy

William IV had not expected to be king. He was the third son of George III and Queen Charlotte, but circumstances beyond his control brought him to the front of the line of succession. William had spent his entire adult life in the British navy. He joined in 1779 as a low-ranking sailor before moving up through the ranks. In 1788, he was given command of his first ship, and in 1789, he was made a rear admiral and named the Duke of Clarence. William's reputation was not distinguished, however. His family had nicknamed him "Silly Billy" because he seemed a likable fool.

He retired from the navy in 1790 and in the same year, began a relationship with an actress named Dorothea Bland, who used the stage name "Mrs. Jordan." Over the next several years, they had 10 children together, all of whom took the last name of FitzClarence. Because the children were born out of wedlock, none of them were in line for the throne. When George IV's daughter died

in 1817, both William and his brother Frederick sought legitimate marriages to continue the family line. Dorothea Bland had died in 1816, and in 1818, William married Adelaide, the eldest daughter of the German Duke of Saxe-Meiningen. William was 52; Adelaide was 25. None of their children, however, survived infancy.

When it became apparent that William was next in line for the throne, he took great care to maintain his health, and when George IV's servant announced the king's death, William could scarcely contain his glee.

From the beginning, he took his role seriously. First, he refused to have an expensive coronation, which made him popular among his subjects. He also worked overtime to take care of business that his brother had ignored.

William was not, however, a skilled politician, and he clashed with Parliament over a variety of issues. He defied members of the House of Lords in 1832 over legislation designed to reform the House of Commons' election process, which was outdated and subject to abuse. The king did not like the reform, and the majority of the lords were against it also. However, William realized that it was in the nation's best interest and convinced the lords not to vote against it. Additional social legislation regulated child labor and abolished slavery in British colonies.

Despite his accomplishments, at the heart of William's reign was his feeling that he was merely a caretaker. His heir apparent was the daughter of his younger brother, the Duke of Kent, who had died in 1820. The duke's daughter, Victoria, had been born in 1819 and never knew her father. William never got along with Victoria's mother, and he was determined to live long enough for Victoria to turn 18, so that she would be old enough to rule without her mother as regent. He got his wish; when he died in June 1837, Victoria was one month past her 18th birthday.

Throughout the years, the monarchy had changed from one in which the monarch's word was law to one where the monarch merely advised and could be overruled. William IV, the last of the Hanoverian kings, understood his role in this evolution. He said, "I have my view of things, and I tell them to my ministers. If they do not adopt them, I cannot help it. I have done my duty."[23]

Chapter Six

THE HOUSE OF SAXE-COBURG-GOTHA

When Queen Victoria took power after William's death, it began a 63-year reign—the longest in Great Britain's history up to that point—that took the British Empire to unparalleled heights. During Victoria's reign, the British Empire expanded to include colonies in Africa, India, Australia, New Zealand, Canada, Bermuda, and countless islands across the seas.

However, when Victoria ascended to the throne, the monarchy had gone through troubled times, and there was little trust. As an institution, the monarchy had gotten a reputation for not helping citizens. According to Mike Ashley, although there had been some attempts at reforms to help the underprivileged, "the Hanoverian dynasty ... had shown little interest in such progress. There was a general attitude of 'Why bother?' amongst both the royal family and many leading politicians."[24] It would be Victoria's mission—and her legacy—to change that.

Victoria's Ascension to the Throne

During the scramble to produce heirs in the wake of Princess Charlotte's death in 1817, George III's fourth son, Edward Augustus, the Duke of Kent, had married Mary Louise Victoria, the daughter of Franz I, the German Duke of Saxe-Coburg-Saalfeld, in 1818. She was recently widowed, with a son and a daughter. Her brother was Prince Leopold, the husband of the late Princess Charlotte. The couple had one child together, born in 1819; they wanted to christen their daughter Victoire Georgina Alexandrina Charlotte Augusta, but the prince regent insisted that she be called Alexandrina Victoria, in honor of her godfather, Czar Alexander I of Russia. The family, however, always called her Victoria.

Victoria was well educated, but somewhat isolated. Her parents kept her apart from other children and especially away from the household of her uncle, the king, fearing that William's illegitimate sons and daughters would be a poor influence on Victoria.

Shortly after Victoria's 18th birthday, William IV died. In her journal, Victoria recorded how she learned the news on June 20, 1837:

> I was awoke at 6 o'clock by Mamma, who told me that the Archbishop of Canterbury and Lord Conyngham were here, and wished to see me. I got out of bed and went into my sitting-room (only in my dressing-gown), and alone, and saw them. Lord Conyngham (the Lord Chamberlain) then acquainted me that my poor Uncle, the King, was no more, and had expired at 12 minutes past 2 this morning, and consequently that I am Queen …
>
> Since it has pleased Providence to place me in this station, I shall do my utmost to fulfill my duty towards my country; I am very young and perhaps in many, though not in all things, inexperienced, but I am sure that very few have more real good-will and more real desire to do what is fit and right than I have.[25]

Victoria's coronation took place on June 28, 1838, with London's citizens lining the procession route to glimpse the new queen. She later noted in her journal that because there had not been enough practice before the event, there were a number of errors, particularly among the clergy. She described how a ceremonial ring was placed on the wrong finger and that "the consequence was that I had the greatest difficulty to take it off again, which I at last did with great pain."[26]

Early Days of Victoria's Reign

Despite the ceremonial stumbles of the coronation, Victoria's reign began smoothly, to the pleasant surprise of many leaders in the government. The new queen was a refreshing change from her three immediate Hanoverian predecessors. The kings had been middle-aged and prone to fits of temper. Victoria, on the other hand, was young, calm, and composed.

During the first year of her reign, Victoria was guided by her uncle Leopold, who had become king of Belgium in 1831. He sent her long letters full of advice about the challenges of being a constitutional monarch, including recommendations not to surrender to Parliament any more powers that had been reserved for the monarch.

Victoria also received help from the prime minister, Lord Melbourne, who offered day-to-day advice on practical matters and filled her in on the history of the monarchy. When Melbourne announced his resignation as prime minister in 1839, Victoria was obliged to invite Sir Robert Peel, leader of the Conservative Party (or Tories), to form a new government since his party had carried the elections. She had not liked Peel before becoming queen but came to respect him because of Melbourne's influence. During the negotiations over the formation of the new government, Peel insisted on following tradition concerning the queen's ladies-in-waiting. Peel wanted the current ladies—who were members of the Whig party—to be replaced by Tories, as a sign of confidence in the new government. Victoria refused, saying she never spoke of politics with the women, but as a result, Peel declined to become prime minister, and Melbourne remained prime minister for the next two years. Although Victoria had won, when Peel's party succeeded in the next elections, she reconsidered her stance. According to historian Jasper Ridley, "Queen Victoria's victory was only temporary, because never again did she challenge the principle that officers of the royal household should change with the government."[27]

Queen Victoria ascended to the throne at just 18 years old.

While Victoria valued Melbourne's advice about many things related to government, she learned that they did not see eye-to-eye on what she considered an important issue. She understood that many Britons were poor, and she wanted the government to help them. Melbourne believed it was not the government's business. However, the young queen soon found someone who shared her interests in social causes, and he became the most important person in her life.

Victoria and Prince Albert

Victoria first met Prince Albert of the German duchy of Saxe-Coburg-Gotha when his father, her uncle Ernest, brought him to England in 1836. He was three months younger than the princess, and she was smitten with him from the beginning.

A few years later, Victoria asked him to marry her, and he accepted. Their wedding took place in February 1840, and with their marriage, the name Saxe-Coburg-Gotha came into the British royal family. The queen remained part of the House of Hanover, but the couple's nine children were members of the House of Saxe-Coburg-Gotha. Their first child, Princess Victoria, was born in 1840; their second, Edward, the Prince of Wales, was born in 1841. Three boys and four girls followed.

Victoria and Albert believed that they should set an example for the kingdom through good behavior that did not result in scandal or gossip. They also shared an interest in social issues, such as the welfare of children and workers in the rapidly industrializing nation. Many of the landmark accomplishments during Victoria's reign, such as improved standards in education, workplace safety, and public health, were the result of her and Albert's views on ways to improve British society. Additional reforms targeted elections as the secret ballot was introduced and voting eligibility was expanded, although Victoria opposed movements to grant women the right to vote.

Life After Albert

Victoria and Albert were an effective team in public and a happy couple in private. Thus, when Albert died in 1861 at only 42 years old, Victoria was devastated. She grieved for Albert for the rest of her long life, always dressing in the black of mourning. Immediately after his death, she retreated from public life. She refused to make public appearances, and she and her children spent extended periods of time away from London.

Although she was out of the public eye, Victoria did not neglect her royal duties. During her withdrawal from public life, she stayed in touch with her prime ministers. Her relationships with them, however, were not always friendly because they pressed her to appear in public more often.

The end of Victoria's seclusion, however, was due less to the prodding of

Victoria and Albert had seen how scandals could damage the monarchy and made it their goal to set a good example for the kingdom.

THE GREAT EXHIBITION

On May 1, 1851, Queen Victoria and Prince Albert arrived in London's Hyde Park to officially open the Great Exhibition of the Works of Industry of All Nations. Albert was president of the commission that had planned the event. They intended it to be an international showcase of the benefits of progress, free trade, and international good will. The fair emphasized the manufacturing prowess of the British Empire, but it also featured art and technological wonders from around the world.

The heart of the Great Exhibition was the Crystal Palace, a soaring, four-level iron and glass greenhouse that covered 26 acres (10.5 ha) of the park. Visitors from all over the world flocked to see it. By the time the exhibition closed on October 11, it had been seen by around 6 million people, many of whom returned several times. The queen herself visited more than 30 times.

The Crystal Palace was the centerpiece attraction of the Great Exhibition in 1851.

her ministers than to a family crisis. In November 1871, Edward, the Prince of Wales, came down with typhoid fever. As the 10th anniversary of Albert's death approached, the prince's prognosis was still uncertain. However, he eventually improved, and the following February, Victoria and the prince attended a public parade through London and a service of thanksgiving for his recovery. The welcome she received from the cheering crowds perhaps did more to convince her to return to public life than the efforts of her ministers.

Over the next 15 years, her popularity soared even more as Britain's wealth and status in the world grew. Victoria's dominions stretched across the globe. A complex and finely tuned network of British ships and railroads brought raw materials from colonies on six continents to factories across Britain. Manufactured goods from toys to textiles to tools were then exported to markets around the world. Despite being involved in a number of wars during Victoria's reign, Britain emerged largely victorious. According to Ashley, "At that time … it would have seemed to Victoria's subjects that Britain ruled the world."[28]

The Victorian Age Ends

Victoria celebrated 50 years on the throne in 1887 with a series of celebrations called the Golden Jubilee. Ten years later came her Diamond Jubilee. She had surpassed George III's record for the longest-reigning British monarch.

She was now in her late 70s and continued to write in her journal every day. However, by 1900, she was suffering from a series of age-related infirmities. Cataracts clouded her eyesight, and her movements were hindered by rheumatism.

As had been her custom since Albert's death, Victoria spent the Christmas of 1900 at Osborne House, her retreat on the Isle of Wight off the south coast of England. On January 12, 1901, she wrote in her journal that she had enjoyed an hour's drive around the island. Less than a week later, she no longer had the energy to continue the journal she had kept for 69 years. She died on January 22, 1901, at 81 years old.

At the time of her death, Victoria was the only monarch most Britons had ever known. She was considered the grandmother of Europe. Through her and Albert's children, she was connected to the leading ruling houses of the era. Her daughter Victoria was the mother of Kaiser Wilhelm II, the emperor of the German Empire and the king of Prussia. Her second daughter, Alice, was the mother of the wife of Czar Nicholas II, the emperor of Russia. Upon her death, Victoria and Albert's son Edward, the former Prince of Wales, became head of the House of Saxe-Coburg-Gotha and king of the British Empire.

Edward VII

Upon Victoria's death, the Prince of Wales became King Edward VII. He was nearly 60. When Edward was a child

Edward VII, shown here at his coronation, was king for nearly 10 years until his death in 1910.

and young adult, his parents had kept him out of royal politics. Although he represented the crown on tours through Europe, Canada, and the United States as a teenager and through India in 1875 and 1876, the majority of his duties involved attending ceremonies at the openings of buildings, bridges, and other public landmarks. He became a popular figure in society through his extensive traveling.

After Albert's death and during Victoria's withdrawal from the public spotlight, Edward had carried on as usual. He married Princess Alexandra of Denmark in 1863 and played an important part in the planning and preparations of Victoria's Golden and Diamond Jubilees. During his mother's final illness, he was at her side along with his nephew, Kaiser Wilhelm II. The empire welcomed Edward as king, and his coronation was a magnificent affair, attended by government representatives from all over the world.

As with Victoria's reign, major advances in the welfare of British society marked Edward's time on the throne, which was later called the Edwardian era. The government passed legislation that made trade unions legal, implemented a program of national insurance, and established pensions for the elderly. The king, however, took little personal interest in such matters. He was more interested in foreign affairs, an interest that had been kindled during his extensive visits abroad as the Prince of Wales.

One of the hallmarks of Edward's reign was his effort to promote good will among the nations of Europe. He succeeded in continuing the positive relations with France that Victoria had

EDWARD VII'S FUNERAL

Edward VII's death in 1910 was mourned across the world; the black crepe fabric of mourning adorned windows and lampposts from Paris to Tokyo. Britons wishing to pay their final respects endured drenching rains and lines 5 miles (8 km) long to pass by the late king as he lay in state at Westminster Hall.

The king's funeral on May 20 brought together one of the largest gatherings of European royalty ever. The gun carriage bearing his casket was followed by his horse and by his dog, a Wire Fox Terrier named Caesar. Three men followed on horseback: the new king, George V; the Duke of Connaught; and the late king's nephew, Kaiser Wilhelm II. The late king's widow, her children, and the new king's wife and family followed in carriages. Other carriages carried five heirs apparent, seven current or widowed queens, 40 imperial or royal highnesses, and representatives from nations around the world, including U.S. president Theodore Roosevelt.

begun, leading to the *Entente Cordiale* (friendly agreement) between the two nations in 1904. He made state visits to Paris, France; Athens, Greece; Oslo, Norway; and Stockholm, Sweden, and met with his nephew Czar Nicholas II at the Baltic seaport of Tallinn in 1908.

His efforts to maintain friendly relations with other countries led to his nickname, Edward the Peacemaker. However, his overtures were less well received in Germany, where his nephew, the kaiser, believed Edward's proposed agreements would threaten German interests in trade, colonial expansion, and international relations. This growing anti-British animosity in Germany would come to a head in the coming decade.

Edward, however, did not live to see these events come to pass. He died on May 6, 1910, at 68 years old. His eldest son, Albert, had died from pneumonia in 1892 in his late 20s, so the throne passed to his second son, now King George V.

THE REIGN OF THE WINDSORS

The death of Edward VII and George V's ascension to the throne ended the House of Saxe-Coburg-Gotha and began the House of Windsor, which remains in power in the 21st century. Throughout the last century, the monarchy has continued to evolve, with members of the royal family sometimes challenging the long-established rules—and role—of the monarchy.

The Reign of George V

A test of George V's leadership skills came in 1914 with the outbreak of World War I, and he rose to the challenge. Great Britain was allied with Russia, where George's cousin, Nicholas II, was czar, but was against his cousin Kaiser Wilhelm II of Germany.

George and his wife, Queen Mary, made an effort to identify with the hardship being felt throughout Britain. They shared the same food rationing as their subjects. During the four years of the war, George made hundreds of visits to army and navy installations, field hospitals, and factories, helping to further the war effort and to boost morale. He said to the troops on the front lines, "I cannot share your hardships, but my heart is with you every hour of the day."[29]

Britain and its allies won the war, but the postwar years brought new challenges. One was the question of Irish independence. Ireland had been under varying degrees of English and then British control for centuries, and many Irish were tired of it. In 1916, anti-British militants led an uprising which was crushed by the British army, resulting in further calls for freedom from royal rule. In the 1918 Parliamentary elections, the Sinn Féin party, which advocated independence from Great Britain, won sweeping victories throughout Ireland. The new members refused to attend Parliament and instead created their own legislature in the city of

ADOPTING THE NAME OF WINDSOR

During World War I, King George V's House of Saxe-Coburg-Gotha had an image problem. The savagery of the war had created an intense hatred of all things German. Stores with German-sounding names were looted, and individuals with Germanic last names were suspected of spying for the enemy. These attitudes even extended to the royal family: The German nobleman Prince Louis of Battenburg, a cousin of the king, was harassed into resigning his post as an officer in the British navy.

On July 17, 1917, King George addressed the problem with a royal proclamation that declared,

> *Now, therefore, We, out of Our Royal Will and Authority, do hereby declare and announce that as from [this] date … Our House and Family shall be styled and known as the House and Family of Windsor, and that all the descendants in the male line of Our said Grandmother Queen Victoria who are subjects of these Realms, other than female descendants who may marry or may have married, shall bear the said Name of Windsor.*[1]

The new name came from the iconic Windsor Castle and remains the name of the royal family to this day.

1. *London Gazette*, July 17, 1917, p. 1. www.thegazette.co.uk/London/issue/30186/page/7119.

Dublin. For the next three years, the Irish Republican Army (which was in favor of independence) and the Royal Irish Constabulary (of the British government) fought each other in guerrilla campaigns of assassinations, bombings, and street fighting. Finally, in 1921, the majority of Ireland became independent, although six counties in the north chose to stay with Britain as the province of Northern Ireland.

Technological advances were changing how people related to one another, and the monarchy was no exception. On December 25, 1932, in an effort to reach out to the people of Great Britain, George V made a Christmas radio broadcast to the nation and the empire. It began a tradition that continues to this day. These messages, as well as newsreels of George and Mary shown in theaters, helped connect the monarchy to the people as never before.

By the mid-1930s, the king's health

was declining, and he died on January 20, 1936. He had seen his country through a world war, social upheaval, and economic turbulence, and today he is considered one of Britain's most important kings. His son David, the Prince of Wales, succeeded him.

The Short Reign of Edward VIII

Edward VIII, known as David to his family, was born on June 23, 1894. He became the House of Windsor's Prince of Wales in 1911 and served in the army during World War I. After the war, he toured the United States, Canada, Australia, New Zealand, and India to help promote goodwill and international relations. The international press found him dashing and outspoken and reported his every move.

On a tour of the United States in 1931, he met a woman named Wallis Simpson, who had been divorced from her first husband, married again, and was now in the process of divorcing her second husband. By 1935, the two were in love, but the prince knew his father would not approve and never told him about the relationship.

When George V died, only a few people knew about Edward's relationship with Wallis, but by the summer of 1936, his affair was common knowledge. The new king, who called himself Edward VIII, believed that the British would accept an American as queen, even though she was now twice-divorced and both husbands were still living. Edward's mother, the former Queen Mary, along with the Archbishop of Canterbury and members of the government, disagreed. They tried to get him to end the relationship.

In October 1936, the prime minister, Stanley Baldwin, gave Edward a collection of press clippings from around the world, documenting the affair. Baldwin pointed out that a king under a constitutional monarchy was more dependent on integrity and goodwill than ever before and that Edward's relationship with Wallis threatened that. On November 16, the king informed Baldwin that he was prepared to abdicate, preferring to give up the throne rather than to lose Wallis.

On December 10, Edward carried out his decision to abdicate, and that evening, in a radio broadcast, he told the nation, "I have found it impossible to carry the heavy burden of responsibility and to discharge my duties as king, as I would wish to do, without the help and support of the woman I love."[30] His younger brother Albert, the Duke of York, took over the throne, choosing the name George VI in honor of his father.

A Duty to Lead

As the second son of George and Mary, the new king had received less attention than his older brother David, who had an abundance of charm and good looks. The young Albert suffered from an irritation of the stomach lining called gastritis and walked with leg braces to try to correct his knock-kneed

Edward VIII left the throne to be with the woman he loved, Wallis Simpson. She was a divorced American woman, a fact that would come up again years later with Prince Harry and Meghan Markle.

condition. By the age of eight, he also had developed a stutter in his speech that became extremely pronounced under stress.

In 1922, Albert met Lady Elizabeth Bowles-Lyon. She was not a member of a British or European royal family, but her family traced its roots back to a Welsh prince on one side and a Scots lord on the other. They were married the following year. They had a happy marriage and had two daughters: Elizabeth, born in 1926, and Margaret, born in 1930.

With his wife's support and professional speech therapy, Albert began to manage his stutter. Although he never fully overcame it, he learned techniques to deal with the stress of formal speeches and radio addresses with only minimal difficulty. However, he was not prepared for his brother's abdication, nor was he ready to be king.

Albert felt he had a duty to lead his country as best he could, however. As Britain's new king, now called George VI, he immediately set about learning about the state of the government and, in particular, the state of international affairs, which were rapidly deteriorating throughout Europe. He dearly hoped a diplomatic solution could be found to avoid another European war, but when World War II began, George VI made a radio broadcast on September 3, 1939, to address his people about the challenges ahead. He counseled that "In this grave hour, perhaps the most fateful in our history," the British people needed "to stand calm, firm, and united in this time of trial."[31]

George and Elizabeth were inspired by the examples of his parents, George V and Queen Mary, while leading the nation in a time of war. They chose to stay in London despite German air raids, even after a narrow escape from a bomb that hit Buckingham Palace, where the king was attending a meeting. The king and queen visited the worst-hit areas of the city, and their concern for citizens brought them widespread approval.

The war in Europe came to a close with Germany's surrender on May 7, 1945. That same day, the king made a radio address in which he thanked his people for their efforts but reminded them, "Much hard work awaits us both in the restoration of our own country after the ravages of war, and in helping to restore peace and sanity to a shattered world."[32]

Changes to the Monarchy

The postwar world brought significant changes to the British Empire and the monarchy. The changes had begun in 1931 with the formation of the Commonwealth of Nations, an association of the United Kingdom, Canada, Australia, New Zealand, and South Africa, former British colonies that were now independent. These nations recognized the king as "the symbol of the free association of the Independent Member Nations and as such Head of the Commonwealth,"[33]

From left to right, Princess Elizabeth, Prince Philip, Queen Elizabeth the Queen Mother, King George VI, and Princess Margaret are shown here in the 1940s in a photo celebrating the engagement of Princess Elizabeth to Prince Philip.

yet maintained responsibility for their own governments.

After the war, other territories of the empire desired independence as well. Faced with fierce resistance in India, in 1947, Britain agreed to end British rule there. The territory became two new nations, India and Pakistan. George VI surrendered his title of Emperor of India, and both India and Pakistan joined the Commonwealth to retain ties to the monarchy.

The postwar years also brought changes to the king's family. In 1947, Princess Elizabeth married Philip Mountbatten. Philip, the son of Prince Andrew of Greece, had been raised by his English uncle, Lord Mountbatten. In 1948, Elizabeth and Philip's son Charles was born, followed by a daughter, Anne, in 1950.

The king's health declined in the following years. He saw Elizabeth and Philip off on an overseas goodwill tour in late January 1952, but the couple then learned that the king had died in his sleep on February 6, 1952, at 56 years old. Thrust unexpectedly and unwillingly into the role of king, George VI had succeeded in restoring the image of the monarchy after his brother's abdication and had shown true leadership throughout the war. Now, that mantle of leadership was placed upon the shoulders of his 25-year-old daughter, Elizabeth.

Elizabeth II: The Longest-Reigning Monarch

Princess Elizabeth Alexandra Mary was born on April 21, 1926. As a teenager, she had stayed in London with her parents during the German attacks of World War II. In 1945, at the age of 18, she enlisted in the Auxiliary Territorial Service, the women's branch of the British army at the time, where she learned how to operate and repair vehicles. Her wedding to Philip Mountbatten was broadcast live on the radio for millions of listeners.

After her father's death, she became Queen Elizabeth II on February 6, 1952, although her official coronation did not occur until June 2, 1953. Elizabeth and Philip's second son, Andrew, was born in 1960, and a third, Edward, followed in 1964. The couple's children were the first members of the royal family to be educated outside the home, attending regular schools and universities. It was another example of the continuing evolution of the British monarchy.

During the first decades of Elizabeth's rule, she worked to improve relations among the nations of the Commonwealth. Throughout the 1950s and 1960s, many former territories of the British Empire gained their independence, particularly in Africa. By 1970, the Commonwealth had grown to 32 nations, and as of 2019, there were 53 nations that recognized Elizabeth either as the head of state or as the head of the Commonwealth.

As a young queen, Elizabeth made countless overseas tours to foster goodwill among Commonwealth nations. Even as she aged, in the 2000s, the queen still regularly met with the prime minister to receive updates on government affairs and current issues. Tony Blair, her prime minister from 1997 to 2007, once commented, "What I found to be her most surprising attribute is how streetwise she is. Frequently, throughout my time as prime minister, I was stunned by her total ability to pick up the public mood."[34] Another former prime minister, Sir John Major, agreed, saying, "There's very little she hasn't seen. In my own experience, there's almost nothing that ruffles her."[35]

In 2015, Elizabeth II became England's longest-reigning monarch, breaking the record set by her great-great-grandmother, Victoria. There have been several celebrations commemorating events throughout her reign. In 2012, she celebrated her Diamond Jubilee, which means she spent

60 years on the throne. The year 2017 brought her Sapphire Jubilee, marking 65 years spent on the throne. She was the first British monarch to reach that milestone.

Family Troubles

Over the years, Elizabeth had to juggle the roles and obligations of the

THE QUEEN MOTHER

One of the iconic figures of the British monarchy in the last century was Queen Elizabeth, the Queen Mother. She was the widow of King George VI and mother of Queen Elizabeth II. After her daughter's ascension, Elizabeth represented the crown during special ceremonies, such as dedicating monuments or opening events, which she continued throughout her long life.

The Queen Mother turned 100 years old in August 2000. She received accolades and congratulations from across the kingdom and around the world. Her final public appearance came in November 2001 when she spent three hours touring the aircraft carrier HMS *Ark Royal*. She developed a cold later that month and died peacefully on March 30, 2002, at age 101. Her daughter the queen was at her side.

The Queen Mother's legacy goes far beyond her status as queen consort and mother of the queen. To many Britons, she was their beloved "Queen Mum," popular for her good temperament and wit, and a symbol of Britain's decency and courage.

monarchy with those of her family. As queen and as head of the Church of England, in 1953 she advised her sister, Princess Margaret, that Margaret's planned marriage to a divorced man was against church practices at the time. Margaret eventually married in 1960, but the marriage ended in divorce.

Margaret's divorce came amid accusations of extramarital affairs, which also plagued the marriage of Charles, the Prince of Wales, to Lady Diana Spencer. The prince, 32, and Diana, 20, were married in a highly publicized ceremony on July 29, 1981. The event was broadcast worldwide and was watched by 750 million people. Their first son, Prince William, was born in 1982, and their second, Prince Henry (known as Harry), was born in 1984. However, the marriage began to fray as Charles continued a relationship with Camilla Parker Bowles. Charles and Diana formally separated in 1992, and Elizabeth II was reportedly saddened by the separation.

The year 1992 was particularly trying for the queen. Her daughter, Princess Anne, divorced her husband, Mark Philips, after nearly 20 years of marriage, after it was revealed that Anne was having an affair with a member of the royal staff. Elizabeth's second son, Prince Andrew, separated from his wife, Sarah Ferguson, after less than six years of marriage. In addition, in the fall of 1992, there was a devastating fire at the royal residence at Windsor Castle. Elizabeth summed up the events of the year in a speech at the Guildhall, the ceremonial center of the Corporation of the City of London. She said, "In the words of one of my more sympathetic correspondents, it has turned out to be an annus horribilis,"[36] which, in Latin, means "a horrible year."

There were more public troubles to come. Charles and Diana were unable to reconcile, and after consulting the prime minister and the archbishop of Canterbury about the feasibility of a divorce, Elizabeth sent a letter to Diana. The letter stated that she had consulted with Charles and the archbishop and that she agreed a divorce was necessary. Charles and Diana were formally divorced in 1996, and he married Camilla in 2005.

Diana was killed in an automobile crash in Paris in 1997 while being chased by paparazzi. Her tragic death brought the queen into the spotlight again. Elizabeth and her family chose to mourn privately at her estate in Scotland, Balmoral, where they had been staying when they heard the news. Many people felt the queen should have made a public announcement immediately. The day before Diana's funeral, the queen released a televised statement in tribute to the late princess, and she bowed her head as Diana's casket passed her at the ceremony. It provided a measure of comfort to those who mourned Diana.

SUCCESSION TO THE CROWN ACT

In 2013, the Succession to the Crown Act amended the Bill of Rights and Act of Settlement under which the male heirs ascend to the throne. For hundreds of years, the youngest son could become the reigning monarch over the oldest daughter. With the 2013 act, the succession order changed to one that is decided only by birth order, not gender.

After Queen Elizabeth, Prince Charles is next in line for the throne, and Prince William comes after Charles. If William ascends to the throne, his children will be in line after him—not William's brother Harry. That means Prince William's first child, Prince George, is third in line, Princess Charlotte is fourth in line, and Prince Louis is fifth in line for the throne.

The New Generation

Losing their mother when they were so young was a traumatic experience for Princes William and Harry, made even more difficult since they were constantly in the public spotlight. Today, though, both men have accepted their public responsibilities and seem to have happy, stable personal lives as well.

As of 2019, Prince William and Catherine Middleton, the Duke and Duchess of Cambridge, have three children together, George, Charlotte, and Louis.

The Duke and Duchess of Cambridge travel in support of the queen, but they also are involved with several charitable organizations, particularly those that support young people.

Like other members of the royal family, the Duke and Duchess of Cambridge represent the queen at events around the world and also participate in their own activities and projects based on their interests.

One of Prince William's projects involves conservation and protecting the environment. He has not only funded conservation efforts such as the preservation of natural areas but also the development of environmental education programs. Additionally, Prince William and Prince Harry have established the Royal Foundation, which is the organizing medium for their charitable efforts. Through the Royal Foundation, William founded United for Wildlife in 2014, which brings together seven of the world's most influential conservation organizations to end illegal wildlife trade. In addition, Prince William is focused on issues, such as bullying and homelessness, that deeply affect young people.

The Duchess of Cambridge is also committed to helping young people. As part of her charitable work, she focuses on issues related to children's mental health and emotional well-being, such as how children can suffer long-term effects from addiction, abuse, poverty, and neglect.

Prince Harry and his wife, Meghan Markle, have the titles of Duke and Duchess of Sussex. When Harry married Meghan in May 2018, he broke with long traditions of the monarchy. Meghan has been married before. In addition, she is American and not of royal blood. In fact, Meghan was an actress until she gave up her career when she married Prince Harry.

Although Harry's actions ran counter to established traditions, even his grandmother the queen began bending the rules for the couple, showing her approval of Meghan and also bringing the monarchy into a new era. For example, Meghan spent Christmas with Prince Harry's family even before they were married, and she became an official royal—something that was unheard of previously. In addition, Prince Harry and Meghan were married in May, a month that was previously forbidden

THE CROWN

In 2016, the television show *The Crown* debuted on Netflix. *The Crown* follows the life of Queen Elizabeth II, starting from when she was a princess and getting engaged to Prince Philip. Early in the series, she is shown making the transition to queen and the changes that go along with it. The show became immensely popular as it offered a glimpse—even a somewhat fictionalized one—into the public and private lives of the royals.

As the show covers a wide span of time, the actors who play the members of the royal family have had to change. Seasons one and two of *The Crown* starred Matt Smith, who was well-known for his role as the 11th Doctor in the famous British TV series *Doctor Who*, and Claire Foy. Smith played Prince Philip, and Foy portrayed Queen Elizabeth. In seasons three and four, the actor for Prince Philip changed to Tobias Menzies, and Olivia Colman was cast as Queen Elizabeth.

Peter Morgan, who created the show, thinks the key is to portray the family simply as people like anyone else. "Let's just stop thinking about them as a royal family for just a second and think about them as just a regular family," he said in a 2018 NPR interview. "No family is complete without an embarrassing uncle."[1]

1. Quoted in Dave Davies, "'The Crown' Creator Sees Britain's Royals as 'Just a Regular Family,'" NPR, January 16, 2018. www.npr.org/2018/01/16/578281741/crown-creator-sees-britains-reigning-monarchs-as-just-a-regular-family.9.

The Duke and Duchess of Sussex broke with longstanding traditions when they married.

for royals because it was believed to be unlucky. Prince Charles also walked Meghan down the aisle at the wedding, which Elizabeth II approved.

Although Prince Harry has stated that he supports the monarchy and the difference it can make, he acknowledges that the duties required by the role make it extremely demanding. As the most outspoken royal, he has not hidden the fact that he is happy to be farther down the line of succession. Prince Harry is also vocal about his personal problems, including panic attacks and the pain of losing his mother at such a young age, and getting counseling in order to help him cope with the tragedy. His comments earned praise from many, especially because his public position helps remove the stigma around mental health issues.

Prince Harry also helps with a number of charitable organizations, including Sentebale, which is an organization he started to provide education, health care, and support for children affected by HIV/AIDS or living in extreme poverty. He even took an HIV test live on Facebook in 2017 to reduce the stigma surrounding the disease.

Envisioning Life without a Monarchy

Even with the royal family's work with charitable organizations and its commitment to helping others, there is still increasing discontent from people who believe the institution should be abolished. In addition, many dislike the idea of being ruled by someone who does not even want the position; they point to Prince Harry's comments about being glad to be far down the line of succession as evidence that even some royals are weary of the monarchy's role in society.

Most people state that their main objection to the monarchy is that it concentrates wealth in the hands of the royal family. However, another, more unexpected reason is that the institution is unfair to the royals themselves, expecting them to do certain things or act in certain ways that may run counter to their individual wishes—such as giving up the opportunity for a different career.

The people who call for an end to the monarchy believe that it does not actually represent them and does not serve a useful governmental purpose since the monarch follows the rules delivered by the prime minister. Instead of being ruled by a monarchy under which power is passed down to descendants, people want to elect a head of state so that they can choose someone they believe will truly represent them.

The monarchy has existed for hundreds of years and changing to an entirely new form of government would be an enormously difficult task. It is not impossible, however. A look at how much the British monarchy has evolved, especially within the last 100 years, is proof of that.

Notes

Introduction:
A Sense of Tradition

1. Quoted in Stephanie Elam, "Why Americans Are Obsessed with the British Royal Family," CNN, March 29, 2018. www.cnn.com/2018/03/29/us/royal-wedding-us-interest-meghan-harry-intl/index.html.

2. Quoted in Caroline Bologna, "Here's Why Americans Are so Obsessed with the Royals," *Huffington Post*, last updated May 15, 2018. www.huffpost.com/entry/british-royal-family-obsession_n_5a4b0788e4b025f99e1d0a4b.

3. Quoted in Bologna, "Here's Why Americans Are so Obsessed with the Royals."

Chapter One:
The Monarchy in Medieval England

4. "Alfred 'The Great' (r. 871–899)," Royal.uk, accessed on November 30, 2018. www.royal.uk/alfred-great-r-871-899.

5. Quoted in John Gillingham, "The Angevins: Richard I, 1189–1199," in *The Lives of the Kings & Queens of England*, ed. by Antonia Fraser. Berkeley, CA: University of California Press, 1999, p. 60.

6. Mike Ashley, *A Brief History of British Kings & Queens*. Philadelphia, PA: Running Press, 2008, pp. 136–137.

7. "Henry III (1207–1272)," BBC, accessed on December 1, 2018. www.bbc.co.uk/history/historic_figures/henry_iii_king.shtml.

8. Peter Earle, "The Plantagenets: Henry III, 1216–1272," in *The Lives of the Kings & Queens of England*, p. 78.

Chapter Two:
The Wars of the Roses

9. Ashley, *A Brief History*, p. 170.

10. Miri Rubin, *The Hollow Crown: A History of Britain in the Late Middle Ages*. New York, NY: Penguin, 2005, p. 173.

Chapter Three:
The Tudors

11. Ashley, *A Brief History*, p. 233.

12. Quoted in Leslie Carroll, *Royal Affairs: A Lusty Romp Through the Extramarital Affairs That Rocked the British Monarchy*. New York, NY: New American Library, 2008, p. 81.

13. John Cannon and Ralph Griffiths, *The Oxford Illustrated History of the British Monarchy*. New York, NY: Oxford University Press, 1988, p. 325.

14. Quoted in Emily Sohn, "King Henry VIII's Madness Explained," NBC News, March 11, 2011. www.nbcnews.com/id/42030034/ns/technology_and_science-science/t/king-henry-viiis-madness-explained.

15. Cannon and Griffiths, *The Oxford Illustrated History of the British Monarchy*, p. 330.

Chapter Four:
The Age of the Stuarts

16. Ashley, *A Brief History*, p. 314.

17. Quoted in "William III (r. 1689–1702) and Mary II (r. 1689–1694)," Royal.uk, accessed on January 7, 2019. www.royal.uk/william-and-mary.

18. Quoted in Cannon and Griffiths, *The Oxford Illustrated History of the British Monarchy*, p. 439.

Chapter Five:
The Hanoverian Reign

19. Cannon and Griffiths, *The Oxford Illustrated History of the British Monarchy*, p. 459.

20. Ashley, *A Brief History*, p. 349.

21. Quoted in Cannon and Griffiths, *The Oxford Illustrated History of the British Monarch*, p. 511.

22. Ashley, *A Brief History*, p. 362.

23. Quoted in "William IV (r. 1830–1837)," Royal.uk, accessed on January 8, 2019. www.royal.uk/william-iv.

Chapter Six:
The House of Saxe-Coburg-Gotha

24. Ashley, *A Brief History*, p. 372.

25. Quoted in "Victoria Becomes Queen, 1837," EyeWitness to History, accessed on January 8, 2019. www.eyewitnesstohistory.com/vic.htm.

26. "Extract from the Queen's Journal: Thursday, 28th June 1838," in *The Letters of Queen Victoria: A Selection from Her Majesty's Correspondence Between the Years 1837 and 1861, Volume 1*, ed. by Arthur Christopher Benson and Reginald Baliol Brett Esher. London, UK: John Murray, 1907, p. 157.

27. Jasper Ridley, "The House of Hanover: Victoria, 1837–1901," in *The Lives of the Kings & Queens of England*, p. 301.

28. Ashley, *A Brief History*, p. 380.

Epilogue:
The Reign of the Windsors

29. Quoted in Andrew Roberts, "The House of Windsor: George V, 1910–36," in *The Lives of the Kings & Queens of England*, p. 336.

30. "Edward VIII Abdicates," History TV, accessed on January 8, 2019. www.history.co.uk/this-day-in-history/11-december/edward-viii-abdicates.

31. Quoted in Ben Johnson, "The King's Speech," Historic UK, accessed on January 8, 2019. www.historic-uk.com/HistoryUK/HistoryofBritain/The-Kings-Speech/.

32. "'We Face the Future with Stern Resolve,'" BBC News, May 5, 2005. news.bbc.co.uk/2/hi/uk_news/4515885.stm.

33. "The Commonwealth: Origins of the Commonwealth," Royal.uk, accessed on January 9, 2019. www.royal.uk/commonwealth?page=3&ch=3.

34. Quoted in Robert Hardman, "From the Unwelcome Visitor at the Palace to the Joy of Losing Herself in a Crowd… Robert Hardman Reveals the Private Side of a Thoroughly Modern Monarch," *Daily Mail*, September 25, 2011. www.dailymail.co.uk/news/article-2041776/Queen-Elizabeth-Private-thoroughly-modern-monarch.html.

35. Quoted in Hardman, "From the Unwelcome Visitor at the Palace."

36. Quoted in Andrew Roberts, "The House of Windsor: Elizabeth II, 1952–," in *The Lives of the Kings & Queens of England*, p. 368.

For More Information

Books

Ashdown-Hill, John. *The Mythology of the 'Princes in the Tower.'* Gloucestershire, UK: Amberley Publishing, 2018.

> This book discusses the story of the princes in the tower and what evidence exists that could prove the bones found there belong to the princes. Ashdown-Hill worked with geneticists and scientists to further explore this mystery.

Fry, Plantagenet Somerset. *Kings and Queens of England and Scotland*. New York, NY: DK, 2011.

> This book is a handy pocket reference of the British monarchy with important highlights of each reign.

Grant, R. G. *History of Britain and Ireland: The Definitive Visual Guide*. New York, NY: DK, 2014.

> This is a richly illustrated guide to the monarchy and pivotal events that shaped the history of the British Isles.

Smith, Sally Bedell. *Elizabeth the Queen: The Life of a Modern Monarch*. New York, NY: Random House, 2012.

> This book gives an in-depth look at the queen's daily routine and her life before becoming the monarch.

Weir, Alison. *The Lady in the Tower: The Fall of Anne Boleyn*. London, UK: Ballantine Books, 2010.

> Weir's book focuses on Henry VIII's second wife, Anne Boleyn, and her long imprisonment before her execution.

Websites

The British Monarchy Official Website

www.royal.uk/

> The official website of the royal family has information on kings and queens throughout history as well as recent news. Additionally, the website provides information on the role of the British monarchy in society.

HISTORY: British Royals

www.history.com/tag/british-royals

> This website has numerous articles on the history of the British monarchy, news, and various aspects of the royals' lives.

Twitter: The Royal Family

twitter.com/royalfamily

> The official Twitter account of the royal family has photos, videos, and news so followers can stay up-to-date on the family's actions.

YouTube: The Royal Family

www.youtube.com/user/TheRoyalChannel

> The royals' YouTube channel contains videos of royal visits and information about their official charities and social welfare initiatives.

Index

Picture Credits

Cover Chris Jackson/Chris Jackson/Getty Images; pp. 6–7 (background) HVRIS/Shutterstock.com; pp. 6 (left and middle), 76 Everett Historical/Shutterstock.com; pp. 6 (right), 78 Hulton Archive/Getty Images; pp. 7 (left), 92 Mark Cuthbert/UK Press via Getty Images; p. 7 (right) Pool/Samir Hussein/WireImage/Getty Images; p. 9 Peter Hermes Furian/Shutterstock.com; p. 11 Dominic Lipinski-WPA Pool/Getty Images; p. 12 Anwar Hussein/Getty Images; p. 15 David Benton/Shutterstock.com; p. 18 VCG Wilson/Corbis via Getty Images; p. 19 jorisvo/Shutterstock.com; pp. 21, 28, 37, 75 The Print Collector/Print Collector/Getty Images; p. 26 Patryk Kosmider/Shutterstock.com; p. 31 Christophel Fine Art/UIG via Getty Images; p. 36 Universal History Archive/UIG via Getty Images; p. 41 Stock Montage/Getty Images; p. 42 DeAgostini/Getty Images; p. 46 Historica Graphica Collection/Heritage Images/Getty Images; p. 47 Georgios Kollidas/Shutterstock.com; p. 49 Dennis K. Johnson/Lonely Planet Images/Getty Images; p. 53 sdfharkin/Shutterstock.com; p. 55 Imagno/Getty Images; p. 59 Universal History Archive/Getty Images; p. 60 Robert Alexander/Getty Images; p. 63 Fine Art Images/Heritage Images/Getty Images; p. 65 Ipsumpix/Corbis via Getty Images; p. 67 Dan Charity - WPA Pool/Getty Images; p. 73 Ann Ronan Pictures/Print Collector/Getty Images; p. 84 Ivan Dmitri/Michael Ochs Archives/Getty Images; p. 86 -/AFP/Getty Images; p. 90 Chris Jackson/Getty Images.

About the Author

Nicole Horning has written a number of books for young adults. She holds a bachelor's degree in English and a master's degree in special education from D'Youville College in Buffalo, New York. She lives in Western New York with her cats Khaleesi and Evie and writes and reads in her free time.